Janet's gift is to walk through an ordinary life and have the insight to feel the rainbow of emotions that makes us all human. The stories in this book bring the reader to the understanding that "only love remains, only love we give away," and that seeing this truth is the beginning of a new life.

Sandy Gerry, RN

Crossing the River Sorrow is a memoir of nursing, motherhood and spirituality. Janet Richards has the uncommon talent of writing simply about what is most profound. With ruthless scrutiny, she examines her life's journey towards compassion and wholeness. Her honesty is deeply compelling. I laughed and cried as the Candy Striper who hid in a closet rather than face her hospital chores morphed into the wise, caring woman who all of us would want at our bedside or dinner table.

Keddy Ann Outlaw, book reviewer, librarian/ blogger

Thank you Janet Richards for charting your nursing journey through its many stages: to learning how to deal with whatever comes along, to compassion, to the golden moment of sharing your patients' pain, and to seeing God's presence in that pain. With my six plus decades of being the patient, I rejoice to find a nurse who came to the same epiphany as I. God meets us in the River Sorrow and assures our safe crossing.

Judy Squire, author of *Hi*

*From one nurse
To another... .*

Janet

This book is dedicated to Monty Martin Mcdonald,
who has known his share of sorrow, and touched
me with his resiliency and courage.

Crossing the River Sorrow

One Nurse's Story

JANET RICHARDS

WESTBOW
PRESS
A DIVISION OF THOMAS NELSON

Copyright © 2013 Janet Richards.

All rights reserved. No part of this book may be used or reproduced by
any means, graphic, electronic, or mechanical, including photocopying,
recording, taping or by any information storage retrieval system
without the written permission of the publisher except in the case
of brief quotations embodied in critical articles and reviews.

This book is a work of non-fiction. Unless otherwise noted, the author
and the publisher make no explicit guarantees as to the accuracy of
the information contained in this book and in some cases, names
of people and places have been altered to protect their privacy.

WestBow Press books may be ordered through
booksellers or by contacting:

WestBow Press
A Division of Thomas Nelson
1663 Liberty Drive
Bloomington, IN 47403
www.westbowpress.com
1-(866) 928-1240

Because of the dynamic nature of the Internet, any web addresses or
links contained in this book may have changed since publication and
may no longer be valid. The views expressed in this work are solely those
of the author and do not necessarily reflect the views of the publisher,
and the publisher hereby disclaims any responsibility for them.

Any people depicted in stock imagery provided by Thinkstock are
models, and such images are being used for illustrative purposes only.

Certain stock imagery © Thinkstock.

ISBN: 978-1-4497-9660-0 (sc)
ISBN: 978-1-4497-9659-4 (e)

Library of Congress Control Number: 2013909589

Printed in the United States of America.

WestBow Press rev. date: 6/10/2013

*"I would maintain that thanks are the
highest form of thought and that gratitude
is happiness doubled by wonder."*

C. K. Chesterton

Heartfelt thanks to these mentors for their unwavering encouragement and to all the patients, family and friends, named and unnamed, who have touched my life and contributed to the stories found on these pages. I dedicate this book to them.

Christina Adams	Keddy Outlaw
Sue Benier	Nancy Payne
Mary Clearman Blew	Ernest and Mitzel Prufer
Mrs. Cohen	Dee Richards
Joni Eareckson Tada	Natalie Richards
Albert Gassmann	Neal Richards
Emily Gassmann	Noelle Schulze
Sandy Geery	Tom Richards
Becker Gutsch	Brandon Schrand
Ryan Law	Mary Snell
Dan'l Markum	Judy Squires
Bryce Olstadt	JD Stevens
Rachel Olstadt	Rebecca Waenink

CONCORDIA UNIVERSITY LIBRAR
PORTLAND, OR 97211

Table of Contents

When the voices of children are heard on the green,
And whisperings are in the dale,
The days of my youth rise fresh in my mind
My face turns green and pale.

Then come home, my children, the sun is gone down,
And the dews of night arise;
Your spring and your day are wasted in play,
And your winter and night in disguise.

> *"Nurse's Song"*
> *from Songs of Experience*
> by William Blake

Reclining naked and content in a bathtub at a mineral spa somewhere near Santa Fe, my bliss is interrupted by piercing screams of someone in distress. Reluctantly, I ease out of the warm water and slosh my way through a maze of rooms in the adobe building to investigate. In one dark corner, a frail Indian woman, surrounded by three frantic attendants, struggles in one of the deep tubs in the state of panic. The combination of warm water, weakness, and fear of falling has rendered her unable to lift herself from the deep tub. Without a thought to our mutual nakedness, I step into the bath, lift my elderly sister to safety, and continue on my way. It's the natural thing to do. I'm a nurse.

Naked or not a nurse is always a nurse.

I chose a career in nursing at the age of twenty unmoved by a sense of altruism or strong calling to minister to the sick and wholly unprepared for the implications of my decision. The year was 1970. I craved adventure and was curious about the human body, although not always in a purely scientific way. Swayed by medical television shows and stories gleaned from teen fiction expressly written to lure young girls to the profession, I made an impulsive choice that seemed right. With the Age of Aquarius dawning and science assuming center stage, a career as a nurse seemed full of possibilities. Medicine held a vague promise of access to a special kind of knowledge of things not generally known, the dark mystery of which had both frightened and intrigued me since early childhood. The decision to become a nurse thrust me headlong into a world of loss and suffering. I soon became enlightened.

But this book is more than tales from my life and times as a nurse. It's more than horror stories from the front lines of sick wards of the past or a historical rendition of the decades of change affecting nursing practice. This book is a personal account of one very ordinary woman's plunge from a mostly happy childhood in the 1950s and 1960s into the world of human suffering and her long quest to make peace with some of life's most troubling issues—the problem of pain and the capricious nature of adversity. Its stories tell of her spiritual struggle and the many teachers who helped to point the way.

When I look back to my early days as a nurse, I see a naïve woman dressed in a too-short uniform dress scurrying to care for an unbelievable number of seriously ill people. She's strong, energetic, and eager to please, but on some level way out of her league. Her resiliency and organizational skills mask an artistic nature and a deeper sensitivity that's stifled and never given its due. Medical tasks become her shield and armor as she pushes through, moving quickly, quietly, and unrecognized, past the suffering and pain she never knew existed–swallowing hard and stuffing it.

As I write these words, I recall the insight of author Anne Lamott describing the students from her writing classes in her book *Bird by Bird: Some Instruction on Writing and Life*. Over and over her students told her: "I will not be silenced again." Anne writes: "They were good children who often felt invisible and who saw some awful stuff."

Many people hold that "awful stuff" inside never giving voice to the pain of experience, and the serious questions that come in suffering's wake until circumstances force buried pain to the surface. When those awful feelings rise from the deep— visible, loud, and feeling anything but good—they cry out for attention. What does it all mean?

Tears of grief, forgotten anger, regret, and, sometimes, joy stain each page as personal images of people and situations long submerged in the annals of memory come back in vivid color. These stories—a lifetime of tiny epiphanies morphed together like pixels in a Magic Eye book—have returned again and again over the years, bobbing to consciousness at unexpected times, forcing me to face what they have to say. Says Frederick Nietzsche: "For man cannot learn to forget, but hangs on the past; however far or fast he runs, that chain runs with him."

At times I'm William Blake's nurse, the cynic, standing at the window, feeling the weight of that chain, knowing the darkness and resenting the light. Other times I embrace the heft and breadth of suffering with hope, to view it with hard-won trust, however fragile, in its ultimate redemption.

Here I lay bare the scenes that comprise the collage that is my life as shown through the lens of my very personal search to make peace with some of the hardest conundrums of human existence. In the end I hope to help the reader see some hope in the sadness that so often pervades this life on earth—a light that darkness cannot overcome.

In the process, naked or not, I have become a writer.

Chapter 1

A Sheltered Start

The silence, often of pure innocence,
persuades where speaking fails.

William Shakespeare
The Winter's Tale

This story begins in 1961. I'm eleven years old and my grandmother is dying of lymphoma. Time weighs heavy as I sit in the dreary lobby of a Long Island hospital, life on hold, waiting for my parents to appear through a set of green swinging doors that lead to the elevators. This is just one of many Saturday afternoons spent in lockup. Grandma's been sick a long time.

The hospital's cloudy windows look out onto a sleepy Manhattan side street. Bare trees under muddy skies and eddies of leaves whirling down the lonely sidewalk paint a gloomy picture. An occasional blast of crisp air rouses me from my drowsy daydreams as visitors scurry in and out of the front door.

The waiting room steams with oppressive heat and smells like medicine and overcooked vegetables. Standard metal chairs with green vinyl seats line the room and a coffee table sits in the center, bulging with tattered magazines and volumes of grimy condensed books.

My mind groans and searches for something of interest. Wall patterns formed by chipped plaster, shadows from the ancient, slow ceiling fan, and a menagerie of dusty plants languishing in the corner of the room are all too familiar. An occasional hospital worker passes by, pushing a steel cart covered with cloth. The grating sounds from the cart's wheels rattle off the high ceilings and linoleum floors of the lobby. Employees and visitors hurry in and out. Everyone looks important. Everyone has someplace to go.

On the morning in question I'm wearing a short plaid dress and black-and-white saddle shoes and I move my bare legs back and forth enjoying the feel of my thighs sticking to the plastic chair seat. I drag my feet on the scruffy floor and look up each time the swinging doors squeak and flutter my way, praying my parents will show. I stare at the sign on the wall that reads "No Visitors Under 18."

The world beyond the swinging doors is as large as my imagination, fabricated from television dramas like *Ben Casey* and *Dr. Kildare*. Mental pictures of a kindly doctor leaning over the bed of an ailing patient, a capped nurse in starched white at his side, emerge in the blurry black and white format of an old television set.

I'm a dedicated reader, and popular girls novels of the day offer plenty of fodder. My mind teems with nursing images – Sue Barton, hospital nurse standing over Grandma, offering a sip of cool water and wiping her brow. And Cherry Ames, student nurse in classic garb, passing pills in paper cups. I've followed Nurse Barton's fictional nursing career through seven volumes, and devoured Cherry's adventures as she nursed in a variety of venues, including an airplane, rest home, and even a dude ranch. These are my references.

After what seems like hours the swinging doors open and Mom and Dad appear, their steps slow and their faces melted with sadness. Little information comes forth. It's 1961 and the word cancer is rarely spoken. The hospital is permeated with an ambiance of foreboding. A hush has come down.

As we leave the lobby and head for the car, Grandma waves to us from an eleventh floor window, her fleshy arm flapping, her face pale, and her eyes sunken shadows. I don't know it, but we won't see her again. This sad goodbye is a parting gift, a bittersweet image, a pixel to be filed away in a collage of childhood memories.

Grandma slipped into the hospital and months later slipped out of life.

* * * * * * *

Grandma's illness is one of my few childhood experiences of human pain and loss. In fact, my upbringing as a baby boomer was remarkable for its conspicuous lack of either academic or experiential education related to serious suffering. The zeitgeist of the 1950s and 1960s, combined with the sheltered nature of my home life and my immense good fortune, resulted in glaring deficiencies in my childhood education. A wide swath of knowledge about what it means to be human went wholly unexamined.

Before tell-all talk shows and the bloom of the information age, many children saw little of the painful underbelly of life. The wounds of World War II remained raw, creating a deep longing for order and control, and a resilient hope expressed by a strong faith in happy endings pervaded American culture. The Salk vaccine had recently conquered the scourge of polio, and antibiotics were emerging with the power to cure many illnesses that had previously been fatal. Movies, television shows, and books reflected these recent victories, as well as the triumph of the Allies over the Nazis, and followed a basic formula that embraced a recurrent theme. Superman leaped tall buildings in a single bound to vanquish the bad guys in every episode. A masked Lone Ranger and his sidekick, Tonto, never failed to apprehend the evildoers and bring them to justice. No matter what the calamity, Lassie always came through. This reliability was supremely reassuring after the horrors of the Holocaust and the powerlessness of paralyzing polio.

Many youngsters of this era were protected from the heartaches of life. Adult conversations were often conducted in hushed tones shrouding stories of sex, scandal, and illness in mystery. Television sitcoms like *Leave It to Beaver*, which ran through 1963, presented a sanitized version of suburban America, setting a standard for families that enforced a facade of simple innocence that never faced the harsher realities. Typical episodes dealt with such simplistic problems as Beaver's angst when the bathtub overflowed, Wally and Beaver at odds over the cleanliness of their room, and June's consternation at her son's refusal to eat brussels sprouts. More brazen plots showed bad-boy Eddie changing a grade on his report card, Lumpy teasing Beaver about a neighbor's kiss, and Beaver agonizing over his haircut. This long-running television series never addressed the really hard stuff.

One remarkable exception to this rosy scenario was a 1950's daytime game show called *Queen for a Day*. Using the classic applause meter, contestants were asked to talk publicly about financial and emotional hard times, and tell the audience why they should wear the glittering crown and sable robe as queen for the day. The winner received a bouquet of long-stemmed roses along with prizes needed to make life easier. The harder the circumstances, the higher the applause meter registered in order to determine the unfortunate contestant with the highest score. Women broke down as they told of children with disabilities, overwhelming medical needs, and deserting husbands. I remember watching an episode while home from school, catching a glimpse of the seamier dramas of life that television of this time normally failed to show. I listened with fascination and wonder.

But, like most of my peers, I remained extremely naïve. When the movie *Reefer Madness*, depicting the evils of marijuana, was shown to our seventh grade class in 1964, most of us were clueless. We later asked, "What's marijuana?" Although we were familiar with bomb shelters –my grandmother's neighbors had them in their backyards – few kids my age thought about the implications of the nuclear threat. The Cuban Missile Crisis came and went, and it was only years later that I became aware of the danger it had represented.

My childhood could have been billed as one long episode of *The Lawrence Welk Show*: wholesome and pure, with every player groomed and coifed to perfection. Expectations were solid, standards were high, and a veneer of respectability was greatly valued. My mother, a sturdy *frau* of German heritage, worked hard to maintain our pristine image and to protect her children from the unseemly elements of the cruder world. The evening news remained off limits throughout most of my childhood, and even *Perry Mason*, with its obvious emphasis on homicide, was deemed objectionable. Many nights I found myself sequestered in the kitchen of our modest home straining to hear the forbidden dialogue on the television through yet another set of swinging doors.

But there were certain moments in childhood that provided some preparation for the revelations that lay ahead. In third grade, a student, too sick to come to school, communicated with our class over a loud speaker above the clock. As the teacher droned on, the boy's voice infrequently crackled into the classroom in muffled tones, knocking us out of our stupor. Of course we wondered what was wrong, but an explanation for his plight was never given. Someone said the boy was in a wheelchair and unable to walk. I imagined him small and crumpled at his desk, as he huddled over the microphone, croaking his comments and questions with great difficulty. One day we heard a rumor that his bones were as brittle as potato chips. This phrase evoked a powerful image –one I've since used to describe my aging body.

In grade school, I went with my mother to visit a baby who had been exposed to rubella during pregnancy. The child—blind, deaf, and unable to hold up his head—sat in a metal stroller while our mothers talked. A crimson sore on the bridge of the infant's nose came from his head rocking back and forth on the metal tray of the stroller. The wound was ugly and raw and seemed painful. I stifled the urge to lift his head, pad his nose, and straighten his body, and I later pestered my mother with a number of questions. This level of suffering was shocking and left its own mark on my then nine-year-old mind.

A legless beggar on a rolling platform selling yellow pencils in the subways of New York, a boy named Terry on crutches, dragging stiff legs encased in silver braces up the steps of the school in first grade, and a single evening spent square dancing in the Poconos with a girl who had five missing fingers, all formed forever images in my mind. These scant first-hand experiences of disability and the human suffering were all I knew as a child.

The year I turned sixteen, my mother began to pressure me to become a hospital candy striper. Always highly concerned about my high school curriculum vitae, my parents concluded that a stint as a hospital volunteer would serve as an ideal addition to my resume and make me more marketable for college. High school in New York in the 1960s was highly competitive, and acceptance to an Ivy League school remained an unspoken goal for many of my classmates and of course their parents. Ambition drove most students to spend months studying volumes of old Regents tests, hoping for outstanding scores on the statewide exams. It compelled many to join do-little organizations like the Junior Library Club and the Art Guild. I belonged to Future Teachers of America. The high school yearbook pictures document my membership, but I have no memory of ever attending a meeting.

I recall feeling more than reluctant to sign on as a hospital volunteer. As a teen I often felt overcommitted—shelving books at the public library after school, playing in the orchestra, writing for the school newspaper, and participating in Girl Scout and church activities, not to mention a heavy load of homework and academic pressure. I loved to play tennis and hated giving up my Saturdays for more work indoors. I felt more than a little intimidated by the idea of walking into a hospital to do who knew what just to pad my resume. But, after weeks of protest, I caved to my mother's dream, donned the requisite pink and white striped pinafore, white cotton blouse, and canvas sneakers, and hopped on the bus to Mineola to report for duty as a candy striper. At the time I had no real notion of what this meant.

To my surprise I received no training, no tour of the facility, no chance to express the rampant anxiety and serious misgivings that began gnawing at my psyche. I met with the director of volunteers in a small office, signed papers, and was given a brief description of my assignment as the purveyor of books, magazines, and snacks from the hospital library cart. My duties included stocking the cart, rolling it down the hospital hallways, and offering candy bars and reading materials to the patients recovering in the their rooms.

The director ushered me to a musty basement storage area and left. The heavy wooden cart I would be pushing was stored in this tiny, unlocked room illuminated by a slit of dusty light coming from a narrow window in a corner under a ceiling covered with ducts and pipes. Tall stacks of well-worn paperbacks and magazines lined the floor, dwarfing a small desk at the center. I loaded the shelves of the painted cart and headed for one of the patient floors.

As the door of the elevator opened, a whiff of strong antiseptic wafted my way. I remember trying to hoist the cumbersome cart out of the lift and feeling my heart in my throat as the wheels caught in the tracks of the door and wouldn't budge. From the safety of the elevator car, I looked down one hallway to the right and tentatively wheeled the cart toward the left, sweaty palms sliding on the wooden push rail as I walked past a few patient rooms. The dark recesses of those rooms teemed with scary possibilities and ominous potential.

Without warning, a horrible fear seized me and flash-froze my Keds in place. This was too much. I knew with all my heart that I didn't want to go inside one of those rooms. Without another thought, I turned the book-laden apparatus around and fled—a gush of relief flowing through my body as I pushed the down button and prayed for the elevator to come.

Before my escape vehicle arrived, a man in a patient gown approached, and I handed him a copy of *LIFE* magazine. This was the one and only piece of reading material I distributed during my long stint as a hospital volunteer. The elevator took me back to the cart storage room, my tiny enclave in the dusty bowels of the hospital. I settled into the chair behind the desk to spend the rest of my shift perusing novels and magazines, and noshing on candy from the cart.

I hunkered down in this haven every Saturday for weeks on end, breaking outside lines I had always been very careful to color inside of–choosing my comfort zone. Week after week for close to a year, I took the bus to the hospital and ensconced myself in this tiny cave, putting in time as a uniformed candy-striper-in-hiding, never stepping out to grace the patient care floors again. Unsupervised, it was easy to do.

Many months later, while walking past the volunteer office on the way to my hideaway, someone on staff asked my name. No one knew me. No one remembered ever seeing me. I introduced myself, mumbled something about the library cart, and slithered out of the building—my days as a bogus candy striper tapering to an abrupt close. I had no intention of ever voluntarily setting foot in a hospital again. At this point, a career as a nurse was the furthest thing from my mind.

Chapter 2

Salad Days

My salad days,
When I was green in judgment:
cold in blood.

Antony and Cleopatra
by William Shakespeare

I t's strange how mystery entices. How the man or woman who plays hard-to-get is the one who pervades our thoughts, the object of our most passionate affections. The things we can't have are often those we most desire. The forbidden door, with its aura of mystery and subtle risk, becomes the one we yearn to open. So it was for me, during my sophomore year in college, when the dark and foreboding ambiance of the patient room became supremely alluring. Somewhere between the ages of sixteen and twenty, adventure and fantasy triumphed over fear, and medicine's vague promise of access to a special kind of knowledge of things not generally known, which had frightened me since childhood, inexplicably morphed into intrigue. My experience as a recalcitrant candy striper was history. Young, short on insight, easily influenced, and ripe for adventure of any kind, I acted on impulse. Unaware of subtle aspects of my personality that influenced my decision and swayed fate, I forged ahead. The swinging door beckoned.

My years in high school on Long Island were happy ones. Teenage life sped past in a blur of activity. My school focused on preparing the college-bound, and as a junior I met with a guidance counselor, as did most of my peers, to begin charting my future academic course. When the advisor casually mentioned a career in medical technology because of my interest in science, I immediately claimed it as my future path.

Several years later, when pressured to declare a major, there was only one thing I was sure of—it wouldn't be medical technology. During a college biology course I found looking into a microscope with both eyes open physically impossible, and deemed the diligence and tedium required to examine minute cells intolerable. I thrived on social contact and attention to detail was not my strong suit. I hated math. The idea of spending my life counting cells on a slide seemed akin to torture. When I faced these realities the goal I'd stated for years evaporated.

One morning after a college chemistry class in a large auditorium, I overheard some women talking about going to nursing school. Suddenly a career as a nurse sparkled with prestige and the exciting experiences I wanted. Even if it wasn't technology, it was still medical, and I remember thinking how my parents would approve. A career in medicine would provide opportunities to help people on the frontiers of new knowledge. The choice was made in an instant, and I left that auditorium with a firm plan.

It's difficult to believe that a single overheard conversation would have such influence. It's even harder to believe that I made the decision as flippantly as I might choose a book from the library or an item off the menu at McDonalds. In subsequent years I would blame the books I'd read as a child—the nursing novels expressly written to lure young women to the profession—as well as the episodes of medical dramas like *Dr.*

Kildare. I'd fault the narrow choices offered to the young girls of my generation—nursing, teaching, and secretarial jobs—to the exclusion of other options. But in the end I realized that although each of these made a contribution, a truer picture of why I chose to be a nurse goes far beyond my quest for adventure and learning. The issue was much more complex.

Many people have speculated based on anecdotal evidence, that the adoption of the role of "responsible child" in a dysfunctional family is the precursor to a career in the helping professions. I certainly fit that bill. Although my stoic mother outwardly controlled her children with a number of unyielding rules and demands, she was passively dependent, and her veneer of confidence frequently crumbled in the face of the many challenging situations that arose in the course of ordinary adult life. In times of crisis, I was my mother's go-to-girl.

As a housewife in the 1950s and 1960s, Mother spent her days cleaning and caring for children alone in a suburban setting. She had little support. My engineer father traveled on business, and, on the rare occasions Dad was home, he remained largely unavailable—engrossed in the television, needing space with his newspaper and cigars, or zoning out on alcohol in a green plastic recliner in a corner of the living room. He'd become accustomed to the three-martini business lunches that were so in vogue during this era, and Manhattans increasingly became his solace as a way to unwind at the end of the day. When problems came up, my mother usually turned to me. As the oldest of three children and prone to taking responsibility, I was the natural choice.

In 1960, as Hurricane Donna approached Long Island, mother worried that our Volkswagen Beetle might be damaged by the storm. She didn't drive, and, as usual, Dad was gone. Not wanting to leave the small car subject to the elements, she told me, then barely ten, to drive the car into the garage. Mother watched from a picture window in the living room as, keys in hand, I headed out in the heavy rain. Looking back on this memory, her request seems insane. As a sheltered young girl, I'd never even so much as touched the steering wheel of a car and had no idea how to drive. Amazingly I was able to start the motor and maneuver the vehicle into the narrow space without incident. This experience remains the quintessential example of my role in the family of my childhood.

There was a reason for my mother's childlike dependency. Her parents, Mitzel and Ernest, who emigrated from Austria and Germany in the early 1900s, still communicated mostly in German (my mother's only language until she was six), which left them socially isolated and dependent on family. Mom remained devoted to her parents and phoned them several times a day. Mitzel and Ernest pulled into the driveway of our house nearly every afternoon, their bulky frames lumbering out of the car with shopping bags full of plastic containers stuffed with old world dishes that my grandmother relished—cucumbers and onions in sour cream, red cabbage, and cow's tongue sandwiches. They often stopped at Horn & Hardart or a favorite bakery or delicatessen in Queens on their way to our house to buy sticky buns or other goodies for after-school treats. Mother rarely baked and professed an aversion to cooking. My grandmother, on the other hand, lived to cook and Mother relied on her to keep the family fed.

Grandma Mitzel stood four feet nine inches tall, a stubby volcano of a woman in a jewel-toned babushka, typifying the proverbial Jewish-mother-gone-rampant, and her guileless effervescence often threatened to blow at the most inopportune moments. Whatever Grandma had could be yours for the asking, and still yours even if you didn't ask. This included her opinions. Loose thoughts, as flaccid as the skin on her fleshy arms, jiggled free at the slightest provocation. Emotional tirades tumbled from her lips, despite our earnest pleas and attempts to keep the peace. Her babbling rants had a predictable pattern: repetitive thought expressed over and over without respite. She embarrassed the family with her forthright outbursts in public places, immature requests, and angst-filled diatribes delivered in loud staccato, which my mother deemed nuts but tolerated without retort. In fact, none of us complained. We'd all learned at an early age that trying to stop her only made things worse.

Around the age of eight, I remember questioning my mother about my grandmother's repetitious rhetoric, labile emotions, and her judgment as a babysitter. When she watched us children it seemed like no one cared. We ran free through the house and the surrounding property. With unlimited access to the refrigerator, we spent our days at Grandma's feasting on ice cream sodas made with ginger ale, butter cookies, and whatever else struck our culinary fancy –generally pigging out. Accustomed to my mother's rigid rules, this just didn't feel okay. At home we were allowed only fruit between meals, and the refrigerator was my mother's domain. I felt the burden of responsibility for my sisters' safety as they roamed the neighborhood, and I worried about doing what was right. I voiced my concerns but they were never addressed.

Mitzel's childish antics had a strong influence on my mother. Although Mom was emotionally unexpressive, she often exhibited the same childlike helplessness and unreasonable, demanding behavior she'd seen modeled since childhood. When Grandma called with the news of my grandfather's heart attack and death, Mom froze and immediately handed the phone to me and disappeared. She expected me to comfort my hysterical Grandma and to take care of the details. When the car broke down, I was the one who was pressed into action, walking several miles to a phone booth to call a tow truck while Mom hunkered down to wait in the front seat. When the elementary school called because my little sister had gone missing from the kindergarten bus, I was the one Mom turned to for help. From a very young age I took on the role of the family fixer.

One of the most graphic memories of my childhood involves a traumatic experience during a flash flood at a day camp. I was nine years old and my younger sister and I were attending a Girl Scout nature camp on Long Island. As a special treat, the older kids were invited to spend the night at camp after the last day, and I had been looking forward to this overnight experience for weeks. Always frugal, my mother fashioned a make-do sleeping bag from a wool blanket and a black shower curtain with pink flamingos, tied jellyroll style with a rope. I had a Girl Scout canteen and metal mess kit and carried a sit-upon sewn from pink plaid oil cloth stuffed with newspaper that I'd made in Brownies. I was ready.

Heavy drizzle fell on the morning my little sister and I left on the bus. I carried my bedroll up a trail to the wooded campsite, excited for my first experience sleeping under the stars. There were no tents, only flimsy tarps called kitchen-flies by picnic tables under the trees. We set up camp. It continued to rain.

It wasn't long before the gentle downpour turned to a deluge, and adults began worrying and then scurrying. I sensed their panic. Soon frantic voices cried out telling us to evacuate, and our leaders attempted to take control instructing us to pack up and flee. Adults and children alike began to run down the narrow trail-turned-stream with a scary urgency. I waded as fast as I could, torrents of rain pelting my face, a river of water streaming over my knees, mud impeding my speed as I tugged the filthy, saturated mess of my bedroll through the muck and headed for the safety of the bus.

Chaos ensued. Buses destined for east, west, north, and south Long Island took on anyone who came to their doors. Desperate to find my six-year-old sister, I boarded several, scanning the crowd for her little face. When I finally found her, relief washed over me. Soaked to the bone, we huddled together on a hard plastic seat as the bus made the rounds of an interminable chain of Long Island communities delivering wet, shivering children, one by one, to their home towns.

It was dark when the driver dropped us off by the gazebo in front of Our Lady of Victory Catholic Church in downtown Floral Park. No one was there to meet us. My sister and I walked together, dragging a soggy blanket, muddy shower curtain, and a damp mass of newspaper "sit-upon" along the cement sidewalk toward home. My mother smiled but showed no anxiety when we turned up at the front door with our sodden load. Perhaps she felt concern but it wasn't apparent. Not to worry: I knew I could manage, and my Mother did, too.

I dealt with my mother's dependencies well during childhood, but not so well as an adult. She relied on me throughout my father's long illness with a cancer-like syndrome related to his heavy smoking, and in her widowhood nothing changed. I knew Mom was suffering, although, true to her nature, she never said so directly. Passive aggressiveness was her mode of communication. Daily phone calls became a problem as she repeatedly tried to contact me at the hospital when I was on duty, and dealing with her calls at work or after a hard day on the job left me pained and empty. I could feel her hurt. Its burden had followed me all through my childhood.

After the birth of my own children, Mother's behavior became more blatantly childish and her visits more difficult. As a young mother on a trip to the grocery with three youngsters under the age of four, I found myself arguing with a much larger sixty-four year-old child who sided with the kids as they cried for candy and toys at the checkout. Mom complained about the food at our house and consistently insisted on her own way despite the disruption that this cause to our family routines— taking a shower when it was time for dinner, demanding to be driven to the store, refusing to wait, pouting and angry. Her demeanor *à la* Mitzel was often that of an unreasonable youngster on the verge of a tantrum.

In the summer of 1991, during a routine phone call, Mom casually mentioned the fact that she'd lost weight. Except for a short period in her twenties, she'd always been obese. The news of her weight loss set off alarms.

"How much have you lost?" I asked with some trepidation.

"Sixty pounds," came the answer. "I haven't been feeling good. The doctor's treating me for depression."

This was the first I'd heard of her health concerns. In her usual passive-aggressive way, she was letting me know that she was very sick.

My sisters and I flew home to meet with her new doctor. A malignant pancreatic tumor, one of the most virulent and fatal types of cancer, had grown way past the point of effective treatment. The doctor advised palliative care—simple pain management. My mother accepted her diagnosis with grace and appeared as stoic as ever as we drove home from the hospital, never letting on the seriousness of what had transpired.

We ate out at Olive Garden that evening, and Mom sucked on lemon drops, too nauseated to eat. This was a woman who loved food, especially onions, of all things. She'd grown up indulging in my gifted grandmother's hearty German cuisine on a daily basis. She once traveled to Europe, keeping a diary that included a record of every lavish meal she had consumed in every single country, to the exclusion of any other details of the trip.

That night in the restaurant, Mom stared at us in silence, vicariously enjoying her children feasting on mixed greens in vinaigrette, spiked with slivers of red onion. I felt the utter sadness of this scene in my own gut. Once again, her needs echoed in my own soul. This time there was little I could do to help.

For most of my life I felt the weight of my mother's dependency. My sisters, both much younger and clueless, didn't seem to have the strength. I felt strong when I could help and was not easily hurt. Always tough, I bristled at my siblings' sappy sentimentality. They wept at silly movies and carried on about injured animals. I seemed to lack the gene for their maudlin ruminations, and I struggled to understand what all the fuss was about.

Because of this seeming lack of sensitivity, my mother dubbed me "Hard-Hearted Hannah," a moniker that would seem just the antithesis of what one would want in a nurse. As a young woman, I acted too cool to care, and I sometimes felt like that silly name held some truth. But in reality, despite this exterior of toughness, a smoldering tenderness and vulnerability lurked under the surface. I dealt with it by taking action.

The aspects of my personality that led to my mother's perception of me as uncaring, combined with my role in the family, were a powerful combination. They would not only draw me to nursing but also help me deal with difficult people and the many challenges that would arise in my chosen profession. Trained to choke down emotions, medical professionals "cowboy up," press on to the business at hand and "get-her-done," no matter what situation comes down. A personality that can do this is almost a prerequisite for the job. These traits were written in my genes.

And so it came to be. On that day in the auditorium during my sophomore year in college, when my quest for knowledge, the lure of the mysterious, and my innate personality combined with the dynamics of the family of my childhood all came together like pieces of a picture puzzle resulting in an impulsive decision that seemed to fit. I was on my way to experiences I never imagined.

Despite my earlier fears, nursing was my destiny.

Chapter 3

❦

Baptism

There's no where you can be that
isn't where you're meant to be.

Song Lyrics from
All You Need is Love
by John Lennon

My initiation into the world of professional medicine is a baptism by fire. Brimming with bravado, I finally burst through the swinging doors for the first time in September of 1970. My assignment is on the third floor of the hospital, and I feel my heart racing as I ascend the stairs two at a time, my short, tight uniform dress restricting my stride. My first patient's room is a narrow chamber in the center of a long hall. I enter, trailing my instructor. I'm in.

The room's dark and my eyes squint to adjust. A woman, wizened with age and disease, writhes and moans in twisted sheets on a steel cot by the window. Her loose skin, ashen under the fluorescent lights, flutters as she gurgles and coughs. Green and yellow fluids ooze from bulging bags at the foot of the bed. Putrid smells fill the air, replacing scant oxygen.

This patient is dying of cancer, and her ancient body looks

19

delicate—deflated—a brittle skeleton with parachute-like skin. She labors to breathe, eyes closed, seemingly unaware of our presence. The solitary nature of her suffering strikes me. I stand at attention at her bedside as my instructor rattles on.

Suddenly a ripple of nausea hits and rises to my throat as the walls on the periphery begin to turn black and close in. Legs buckling, I head for a chair by the window and fold into it with my head between my knees. There I stay for several minutes, too scared to look up and face my instructor—afraid I'll vomit or pass out, embarrassed by my weakness.

When the world returns in color, I wobble from my seat and head to the door for a quick exit. The instructor follows, but I'm not in the mood to talk. I lean against the wall in the hallway trying to get a handle on what's just transpired. I'd come very close to blacking out. Five minutes into my nursing career I'm ready to call it quits.

* * * * * * *

Routine and familiarity have a way of blurring the edges, and, with the passage of time, the odors and scenes of sickness proved much less jarring. I could do the job. I soon understood that attention to the task at hand and rapt focus on the technical details pertaining to patient care (the input, the output, the medications, the labs) were the tools of choice to fend off the harder aspects of caring for the sick—things that could wreak havoc with objectivity. Activity was the key.

Advances in medicine made the work more complicated, and it's an understatement to say that there was more than enough action to keep me busy. Staff shortages were approaching a crisis during the 1970s, and the workload was staggering often beyond belief. The tasks required to physically care for patients consumed every minute of every shift, and, devoting my energies to the patient's hands-on care, helped me move past uncomfortable feelings.

But the patient's suffering often broke through. Despite earnest attempts to remain objective, my own emotions made themselves known. The screams of patients being treated for massive burns, the horrors of medical interventions gone wrong, and the senseless tragedies and fragile nature of human life all came at me full force. These realities couldn't be escaped. Pain and sorrow took on faces. The river of sorrow and suffering flowed.

Days after nearly fainting, I returned to the same ward to continue my introduction to clinical care. Much less confident than the day before, I shook with the anticipation of what I might be facing. My instructor was all business and met me at the nursing desk to give me the low down. My assignment was a twenty-seven year-old woman with a progressive form of multiple sclerosis (MS). With my sheltered background I'd never even heard of this disease, and I headed for the books to spend the first half hour of the shift reading up on my patient's malady and going over the treatments I would be providing.

Jane was an elementary school teacher who'd recently married and started experiencing the first symptoms of illness shortly after her honeymoon. The disease hit without warning, blazing through her nervous system with a vengeance, destroying the myelin coating of her nerves and compromising neural connections that made up the communication network in her brain and all through her body. Effective treatments for this aggressive form of progressive MS hadn't yet been discovered. In just a matter of weeks, Jane had lost her ability to move at all.

My patient wept softly as I approached to introduce myself. A catheter bag hung at the foot of her bed. Her disheveled hair, sunken eyes, and grotesquely thin frame made her look like a starving street urchin. She rested on her side amidst a mass of white cotton sheets and mounds of pillows, unable to turn over on her own. Her story tumbled out between sobs. She told me about her young marriage, her grief over her deteriorating condition, and her growing fear that her husband might leave.

21

Her anguish came in torrents punctuated by wails of grief. I listened, speechless in the face of her roiling despair. In fact I couldn't speak. I had nothing to offer. Floundering in an attenuated state of panic, I turned to my instructor for advice.

"The patient's emotional lability is a symptom of her illness caused by changes in her nervous system and the demyelization of her neural connections," the instructor opined. "Her immune system is attacking the myelin coating essential for the communication of the nervous system. Obviously the center that controls her inhibitions is affected."

My instructor's assessment, however accurate, did little to help. Yes, Jane had trouble controlling her emotions, but who wouldn't under the circumstances? Explaining the disease process in medical lingo seemed so clinical, so devoid of compassion, so lacking in practical help for Jane or for me.

I would leave the hospital after my shift, able to choose from a tantalizing array of evening activities—a trip to the store, dinner out with friends, maybe a movie. I took my myelin and the mysterious workings of my neurons for granted as I made decisions and moved my body with liquid ease. My patient's losses loomed heavy—her choices disappearing at a maddening rate without recourse. I imagined myself in her place, tethered to the bed, probably for the rest of life, as MS took over nerves, and dreams slipped away.

Humility and shame swept over me – humility for my inability to make things right, and shame for my own good health and the freedom to choose. But I swallowed those feelings and moved on. I'd felt this type of shame in the past. It came before I'd even thought of being a nurse. It left an unforgettable mark during a college visit to an army hospital for veterans returning from Vietnam. As I walked the gauntlet past rows of young men in wheelchairs with stumps and missing body parts, I became painfully aware of the sound of my footsteps on the linoleum floor and I couldn't meet their eyes. I was ashamed of my intact body.

There would be many other patients like Jane. She is the most memorable because she came early, as I was just beginning to see true grief as well as the increasingly uncomfortable reality of human vulnerability and the despair that could result from illness. Nursing school courses, so academic and objective, rarely touched on how to deal with emotions in regard to the random and inequitable nature of human pain. On my second day in the hospital I was already full of questions, but there was nowhere to turn for answers. Although these issues would continue to surface throughout the years of training and beyond, the subject of a caregiver's own emotional health never came up. This was one topic that no teacher ever broached.

Chapter 4

Lone Star Nightmares

Growing up in New York, I never imagined that I would one day be working in a hospital in Texas, but that's exactly where I landed during Christmas vacation in 1971.

My family left Long Island in early 1968, while I was still in high school and just a few months shy of graduating. Needless to say, I begged my parents for a reprieve fervently hoping to live with friends while finishing my senior year, but my protective parents would not relent. As painful as it was to leave the village of my youth, it was even more painful to see where I wound up. The move to the Texas suburbs might just as well have been a move to Iraq.

The town of Floral Park, which had been my home since age six, was an ideal place to grow up. One of the many small communities on Long Island, patched together like quilt squares from Brooklyn to Montauk Point, it had the flavor of a quaint New England burg. Its wholesomeness was symbolized by the fact that all its streets were named after trees and flowers. The town boasted a central square, gazebo, and a downtown complete with Redvanley's Department Store, a family-owned candy shop, a deli, and a delightful German bakery. Located on the cusp of the New York City borough of Queens, just minutes from Manhattan by train, Floral Park offered a small town ambiance with the best of both urban and suburban life.

Our family frequently traveled to New York City to see the Rockettes at Radio City Music Hall, the circus at Madison Square Garden, and to go shopping at Macy's. We treated ourselves to sundaes at Schrafft's ice cream parlor and perused the shops along Park Avenue. We feasted on chestnuts roasting on an open fire from little carts in the street at Christmastime and hot dogs from corner kiosks. Skating at Rockefeller Center under the giant tree and window shopping in downtown Manhattan became treasured holiday traditions.

As teenagers, my friend Alice and I hungered for everything the city had to offer, and the Long Island Rail Road buzzing through Floral Park at regular intervals proved to be our ticket to the cosmopolitan experiences we craved. We took in Joan Baez in concert, the Vienna Boys' Choir, and world-class tennis at Forest Hills, and we frequented the theaters in Chinatown that featured romantic soap operas with English subtitles. On weekends we hung out in Central Park trying to relive scenes from the movie *Breakfast at Tiffany's* and imagine ourselves as urban socialites. Manhattan was our playground.

In contrast, Texas in the 1970s was the land of beauty queens with bouffant hairdos and country cowboys who'd never left Tarrant County. Compared to the high-pressure atmosphere of New York, my Texas high school seemed supremely insipid. Teachers often deserted their classes at the onset, leaving them unattended for entire periods. Putting in the required seat time was all that was needed for a student to get an A. Texas heat was as stifling as the stuffy country club where my parents golfed on weekends. After I left for college, the few holiday vacations and summers spent at my Mom and Dad's house felt like exile on a sterile planet. It wouldn't be the ivy league school I'd dreamed of attending, but acceptance to an out-of-state university proved to be my passport to freedom.

Shortly after beginning the second year of clinical rotation in nursing school, I returned to Texas on winter break, low on funds. Oh how I missed New York. With no real friends in town and dreading the prospect of six weeks in my parent's home, I applied to work as a nurse's aide at a local children's hospital. As a nursing student with extremely limited training in a hospital setting, I had cared for very few patients one-on-one, and even those were under the direct supervision of a teacher. The hospital was still new and scary. I reported to work as a nurse's aide, as green as they come.

The hospital was located in the good old Texas Wild West, and in 1970 it sported its own brand of medical standards to match. Doctors came to work drunk, aides slept on duty, and entire floors of sick children were routinely left under the supervision of untrained personnel. My official job title remained nurse's aide, but my status as "nurse-in-training," combined with a serious shortage of licensed employees, often led to assignments that were far beyond my knowledge and abilities. Although a supervising registered nurse (RN) worked nearby or only one floor away, I frequently found myself alone with too much responsibility. With scant experience to draw on, and too naïve to set limits, it wasn't surprising that I felt perpetually unsure of what I was doing. My experiences at that Texas hospital would provide lots of material for recurrent nightmares.

One evening I answered a call light to find an obese teenage girl lying in a pool of her intestines and other organs. The stitches of her abdominal wound from recent bladder surgery had given way, literally spilling her guts onto the counterpane. The young girl, eyes wide, mouth open in a quiet scream, looked to me for help. I was in charge of the floor. Alone. The real nurse had gone to dinner.

This gory scene shocked me. It seemed unreal, unimaginable—something I had never considered as a complication of surgery. It certainly hadn't been mentioned during the few clinical courses I'd taken in nursing school. I dashed from the room to call for help on the phone, and then ran back to the patient without a clue of what to do. Frantic, I searched the room for a packaged dressing to cover the gaping opening. I tried to stay calm, to reassure the frightened child that I had things under control. It was all an act.

That same night, the care of three teenagers in a ward near the nursing desk fell to me while the evening RN was gone on break. All three boys in the large room had made the horrible mistake of diving into shallow water and had been hospitalized for weeks with broken necks. All three young teens were quadriplegic. I was horrified at the prospect of entering that ward, too scared to face three young men so close to my age in such a desperate condition. Pain seemed to be oozing from behind the closed door. That familiar fear of the dark possibilities of the hospital room festered and rose to consciousness, but this time there was no way to retreat. Much to my relief, the boys never pulled their call lights.

My outlandish responsibilities as a nurse-in-training continued, and things often went wrong. A child bit down on a mercury thermometer. The glass funnel connected to an infant's feeding tube on the top of an incubator shattered when I moved the overhead lamp. Teenage parents of eight-month-old twins with spina bifida and hydrocephalus stood by their children's beds close to tears, obviously scared and devastated by the immense burden of their babies care. They turned to me. Their questions flew at me and over my head. I lacked the knowledge or experience to be of any help.

One evening, working alone on the infant floor, I crumpled into a chair behind the nurses' station. Across from the desk lay a beautiful child in a tiny crib. Earlier that day she'd wandered away from her house unattended and fallen into the family swimming pool. She was an angel with blond curls and a tiny rosebud mouth, unconscious in a deep coma and not expected to survive. I was her nurse.

I could scarcely comprehend the tragedy that had befallen her. Where were her parents? I stood over her crib watching her even breathing. There was no one to talk to, nothing to do, and my painful feelings flowed. I looked down at her perfect little body, full of grief that had no place to go. The image of her sleeping form, so tragic and alone, still brings tears even as I write this.

That summer I learned more than I'd bargained for, and it wasn't all good. Looking back, it was obvious that I too was drowning—a brand new student nurse out of her depth and not smart enough to let anyone know—playing a role, trying to do what was required yet grossly undertrained for the charge given. The troubling emotions experienced in this setting rattled my brain with long-lasting effects. The maintenance of order and control became a holy goal and stuffing emotions a solid routine for coping. This was a survival skill that came easily. Feelings could be crammed away, and activity could take their place. After all, I'd been doing just that sort of thing all through my childhood.

One morning I arrived on the floor to accept my assignment as a fill-in for a licensed nurse who was out sick. This was nothing new. It was early morning, and children were being prepared for surgery. It was time to give two pre-op injections to a pair of siblings scheduled for tonsillectomies. The patients, a toddler, and her ten-year-old brother shared a room. I drew up two vitamin K shots and a big shot of Demerol for the older boy, who was scheduled to go to the operating room first, and bopped down the hall.

Shots were still scary for me at this point, especially injecting medicine into the tiny legs of a baby. We'd been taught about placement to prevent hitting a nerve. Feeling some angst, hands shaking, I gave all three injections and hustled out of the room, intending to go on to the next job at hand. As soon as I stepped into the hallway my stomach tightened in terror.

I hadn't been paying attention! Who got the big shot of Demerol? Did I give the older boy two doses of vitamin K and the younger a lethal dose of narcotic? So worried about technique, I'd injected three shots without considering what they were or who they were for. A large shot of Demerol could have serious consequences for a small child. Wild with panic, I went back to the room and retraced my steps. I remembered that it took longer to inject the big dose of narcotic and that I'd given it to the older boy. I didn't make a mistake. This provided little comfort. I realized how close I'd come.

The experience of the Texas children's hospital changed me, but not for the better. It was there I learned the hated feeling of being out of control, and I vowed to do whatever it took to never let it happen again. From that day forward I never went to work without a black china marker to label syringes with their contents in order to assure myself that I was administering the correct medicine.

But a black china marker wouldn't control the sadness. That vacation job taught me well. From that time forward, I never went to work as a nurse without a lock on my heart.

And so it was that with steel resolve I returned to college that spring, sadder and wiser, yet heady with confidence and ready to tackle the world. The Texas hospital experiences, however traumatic they were at the time, left me with a taste for drama. I'd been to battle. I'd faced active duty – been in the trenches and survived. I felt ready to continue the challenge.

To be honest, nursing school had been disappointing. The in-depth knowledge of the workings of the human body and cutting-edge science hadn't materialized to the extent I expected. In fact, the curriculum, with its long units on the precise way to give a bed bath and make a bed in the Nightingale tradition, were tedious. The basic foundations of nursing care, incorporated from historic precedent, stressed strict protocols for patient hygiene and basic personal care that were covered in such detail and were so ingrained that to this day I still feel immense discomfort if I enter a room where the opening of the pillow case isn't facing away from the doorway.

Assigned to care for one patient under the instruction of the supervisor, I frequently felt like there wasn't enough stimulating information coming my way. After what I'd been through in the Texas hospital, caring for one patient on the floor was too easy, and I felt the need for high drama. Something more challenging seemed in order. I approached my teachers to inquire about a move to intensive care.

Chapter 5

The Plunge

It's 1971 and I am reporting for duty for the second semester of clinical rotation in my second year of nursing school. The Intensive Care (ICU) facility of the hospital where I'm assigned consists of a large room with a central desk. Patient beds line the walls on either side, without amenities. Seldom-used privacy curtains hang limp and the air reeks of iodine and ether. Overhead lights blare night and day. Most of the patients are too sick to walk, talk, or even breathe on their own. There are few dinner trays here. Clothes are optional. The rules of ordinary life just don't apply. At times the humanity of the patient is only an afterthought.

Respirator pistons pound, each one programmed for an occasional sigh, and the steady drone never stops. Nurses, interns, and residents flit about attending to the various tubes, bags, and machines as I stand back watching. The phone rings without mercy demanding attention. There's a clipboard at the end of each bed recanting an often tragic story that's frequently read and discussed. I struggle to process. Even the language is new. Intensive Care seems an out-of-body experience on a foreign planet, and I'm a curious alien taking it all in.

On this first day of duty I feel invisible, like an objective observer hovering somewhere overhead. I look down to see myself lingering at the bedside of a young girl—a college student turned organ donor. The patient's inert form moves only as her chest rises and falls with pressure from the ventilator. Her long dark hair is spread on her pillow, and she appears to be sleeping. Except for the tube in her trachea she looks so normal. I'm told she was engaged to be married, lived in a dorm, and was studying to be a veterinarian. The night of the accident she'd gone out for pizza. Sadness washes over me. Her life is now part of mine. I can't go back.

Every patient in intensive care is splashed in color. A pretty woman in a deep coma was hit by a car in the airport parking lot. She has perfect, polished, pink nails. A teenage boy who grabbed a live wire is asleep with his charcoal arms propped on IV poles; they will soon be amputated at the shoulders. Parents of a handsome young man with red hair and a neatly trimmed beard hover expectantly over the bed of their comatose son. He went to bed with a headache and now his respirator hammers. A badly burned man floats sedated, waiting to die, his swollen body covered with gauze and white cream.

The grief I feel hits me like a sneaker wave. Once again I've become aware of the suffering of life in a way that escaped me for the first two decades of my own. A curtain has parted, but the mystery of medicine that once seemed so attractive has a sharpness that pierces my veneer of control. Feeling heavy, I step out for air and speed toward the front door of the hospital to head for home. I've been a nurse for just a few short months, and the exit sign never looked so good.

* * * * * * *

It may be hard for those born in other eras to understand the shock of a naïve young woman's plunge into the world of pain and trauma that was intensive care in a teaching hospital in the early 1970s. The irony of the Girl Scout motto, "Be prepared," which had been my childhood mantra, soon became apparent. Barely out of the hospital lobby, I'd entered a world of suffering that shook me to the core. Once again I felt unworthy and questioned the seemingly random and inequitable nature of tragedy. The unfortunate souls who'd touched my life in intensive care had no choice but to face their fate. I could go home.

Home during my first year of nursing school was a Tudor-style apartment building across from the school. This was an exclusively female residence that housed nurses-in-training. It was a fun place to be at that time of my life because most of the students in our class lived there for the first two semesters. The apartments were spacious, and the location convenient. The dorm-style atmosphere provided us with a place to talk with our peers and unload at the end of the day, and we spent many late nights in each other's apartments doing just that.

One evening, a bunch of nursing students congregated down the hall at the apartment of a fellow student named Pam. We sat at her kitchen table discussing our impressions of the curriculum and exchanging stories from our work in the hospitals. At some point our conversation turned personal. Pam showed pictures of her fiancé, who was a helicopter pilot in Vietnam, and talked of plans for her upcoming wedding. She told of her parents' acrimonious divorce in 1955, and how it had affected her and her four siblings.

I listened to Pam's stories with interest. Divorce was another one of the experiences I'd missed. Each member of my large extended family remained married to his or her original spouse despite the often painfully apparent absence of marital bliss, but Pam was not so lucky. When she was five, her father left and moved across town to start a new family, forcing her mother to raise their five children (one of them affected by cognitive disability) on her own. The social stigma of divorce during this time only added to the burden.

It was during this evening get-together that Pam talked about her brother Tom, who was a year older than her and just out of the service. He'd volunteered for the army right out of high school at the height of the Vietnam War. Even though I'd grown up in the shadow of WWII, the senseless deaths occurring in Vietnam really hurt. I had a hard time justifying violence as a solution to anything and couldn't imagine volunteering to participate in Viet Nam. I remember thinking: *I would never marry someone like that.*

Sometimes we miss important moments like these, but this one made an impression. That casual conversation during a nursing dorm chat would later return to my mind in ironic detail, if only because of its uncanny foreshadowing of things to come. Of course I didn't know it then, but that bitter divorce that happened so many years ago would have a huge impact on me and my future.

Life is often rife with mystery. The unique collection of people we meet, the circumstances we find ourselves in, and unexpected way things unfold despite our earnest attempts at control, often blindside us with an uncanny feeling that things are happening for a reason – that there's a greater plan. Perhaps we're not seeing the whole picture. Eerie coincidences, synchronistic encounters, and odd epiphanies strike without warning to lead us on new paths and new questions. So it was for me on a fall day in my twenty-first year when one such encounter changed me forever.

Chapter 6

❧

A Special Kind of Knowledge

It's Tuesday, late in the afternoon during the second year of my clinical rotation, and I'm looking out the window on the eighth floor of the hospital. The sky, a hundred shades of dull, looms heavy with the ever-present smog that clogs the urban air. An eerie wind rattles the panes of glass as I peer down on the scene below. I'm watching the cars as they pass under the walkway connecting the medical school with the hospital, and studying the clumps of people shuffling about lost in their own thoughts. I am thinking about my plans for the weekend, and my uncomfortably tight uniform with its high-waisted pinafore and too-narrow neckline that pinches my neck when I move my arms. Mostly, I'm stalling for time.

My feet feel super-glued to the floor. My legs are as heavy as my spirit as I contemplate the task ahead. This is new territory, and my stomach churns. One of my patients from the rotation in ICU has been transferred to a regular room on the neurology floor, and I've come to see her. She's twenty years old and paralyzed.

I was working the day Carrie was admitted to intensive care. Her serious injury resulted from a freak accident during a routine shopping trip on a snowy day. A winter storm had transformed the frosted asphalt into a treacherous plane, and

Carrie's husband's pickup slid on the frozen slick and swerved, slamming her head sideways into the passenger door window, snapping her spine, rendering her body and limbs numb and motionless. Surgery would strengthen, stabilize, and realign broken bones but nothing more. The damage to her spinal cord at the level of her sixth cervical vertebrae happened at the instant of impact. Her paralysis would remain permanent. She had forever lost the use of her legs and hands.

I'd watched Carrie's during the first harrowing hours as she awaited surgery, when everyone was still hoping for the best. As a new student, I was once again a quiet observer, unsure of how to participate as doctors and nurses hustled around her bed administering care. Her young husband also stood by in stunned silence—tears welling, his form slumped against the heater under the window, eyes blazed wild with fear and disbelief as he struggled to make sense of his sudden immersion into the alien world of sickness and disability.

Paralyzed. The facts concerning Carrie's devastating quadriplegia and what it meant took me by surprise. I'd heard of paralysis—Roy Campanella's injury in a 1958 car accident, Jill Kilmont's skiing mishap that hit the newspapers the week her picture was featured on the cover of Sports Illustrated. But the devastating, irreversible nature of their plights never registered. Pressure sores, urinary catheters, bowel programs, and spasms—these were now part of my new and ever-expanding medical vocabulary. This knowledge plunged me into reality from a totally different point of view. Caring for Carrie's broken body over the course of her days in ICU, touching her and being touched by her, was bringing paralysis up close and personal.

At my post by the window that November day, I'm aware of my own fear. I'm scared that the sadness and horror of what's happened to my patient will overwhelm us both—afraid of the places my mind goes without a conscious effort toward restraint. I picture myself in Carrie's place and the terror and despair of being unable to move, feel a touch, or control bowels or bladder, knowing that I never will again. These thoughts are so uncomfortable that I'm compelled to move on. I finally turn and enter the patient's room.

Carrie lies face up and motionless, her passive body sandwiched between the two canvas slings of a metal bed called a Stryker frame. A bag of amber liquid hangs on its side. I bathed her during her long stay in intensive care, and her dark skin, familiar and unblemished, peeks out from an opening at the front of her flowered gown. Her hair is thick and long like mine, but a matted mess from weeks of neglect –her scalp still orange and crudely shaven at the temples where metal tongs pierce her skull to hold her head immobile.

I stand back as two attendants come to turn her—one standing at each end of the bed, counting to three to coordinate a quick flip. Carrie's body shifts slightly with the weight of gravity as the metal frame is turned. Overcome by the sensation of falling, and unable to exert any muscular resistance to alleviate her helplessness, she screams as she's rotated like an animal on a spit, the metal tongs tugging at her temples. One leaden arm falls, and she's powerless to stop it. My own scream is noiseless, caught in my throat, forming a lump that travels to the pit of my already queasy stomach.

Carrie is lying face down now with only time to spend studying the green and white squares of speckled linoleum beneath her face, so I crouch on the floor by her head and look up. She smiles and greets me without a hint of sadness. "My husband's promised me a new wardrobe," she says too quickly, "when I'm up and walking again. Mom's watching the kids."

She pines for her two young children and chats about their activities. She worries that her mother has more work than she can handle. She complains about the hospital food. I listen and nod.

My mind scrambles for a reply, but words sink before they're spoken. Thoughts of wardrobes, activities, and food float like helium balloons up to the tiled ceiling and then drift away. When my silence finally breaks, I succumb to the very human urge to respond to another's suffering by telling about some of my own.

"I broke up with my boyfriend," I offer, regretting the words even as they fall.

For a moment we're quiet. The air seems heavy. This was the wrong thing to say.

"Maybe you'll get back together," she says with flat hope, her face to the floor.

Our eyes meet in uneasy knowing. We live in two different worlds.

Once again I've positioned myself by the window. It's evening, and the cars on the street below have turned on their lights as commuters scurry home—everyone busy, full of plans, activities, and places to go and so unaware of the suffering here. As much as I want it, there will be no happy ending. Nothing can change that.

"I think I am able to move my toes," she says.

Over four decades later I still hear Carrie's voice and recall those words. I see myself at the foot of her bed, glancing out the windows with darkness closing in. I don't know it, but this is a pivotal moment. I turn. Time loses meaning as I stand head bowed, tentatively looking down at the bottoms of my patient's feet. I'm waiting, even hopeful, staring at her bare soles and frozen toes.

Her feet aren't moving.

And then I know. Pain can be palpable as it moves across the space between two people, molten, unrelenting. Like joy and laughter, it's quite contagious. This is the special kind of knowledge I wanted, even craved going into nursing school, and yet it's not at all what I expected.

And this lesson will be repeated again and again and again.

Shared pain is still pain. Some sadness will never let you go.

Chapter 7

☙❦☙

County General

A blast of frigid air hits my face as I exit my Volkswagen Bug and head toward the front door of County General Hospital. It's six a.m., and a garbage truck trundles past. The city's just beginning to wake up, and the darkness looms with possibilities. Scanning for danger, I hustle through the parking lot. The random violence that keeps the post-op surgical floor of County General so busy occurs with disturbing regularity. Caring for its victims is one of my jobs. My eyes dart as I navigate the familiar sidewalk at a fast clip, heading for the entry.

Ducking into an empty elevator, I swoop up to the seventh floor and the doors open with a ding. As usual for this time of day, the parallel halls of our post-surgery unit are unlit and silent—eerily quiet. It's early; the patients are still sleeping.

The familiar swoosh of respirators emanates from the Intensive Care Unit located across from the central desk that lies between the two long halls. A solitary night RN scurries to finish last-minute details, and the rubber soles of her shoes squeak as she tootles down one side of the floor with her flashlight, balancing a tall stack of pleated paper cups filled with pills. Two bleary-eyed aides slump behind the nurse's desk like brooding hens waiting for time to pass. Their weary heads occasionally droop and bob as they fight sleep. Rows of charts with metal covers rest in their racks, waiting for action. There are no doctors in sight. This is the eye of the storm, the calm before the tempest.

My first stop is a giant urn of coffee in the break room behind the nurse's station. The yellowed walls of this dingy room are lined with dented lockers, and I toss my purse into one in the corner and grab a ceramic cup from a pile by the sink. I'm already in a hurry.

The room smells of cooked coffee and cigarettes. A dilapidated card table surrounded by four folding chairs sits in the center, dominated by a humongous ash tray, full to the brim. This is the station where staff members go to self-medicate. A quick smoke here will be the only break in the action for many. There'll be no time for rest in this windowless enclave, no leisurely lunch or idle chatter with co-workers. Caffeine is my drug of choice. I'll be back only to fill my bottomless mug with some of the strong brew and for a visit to the bathroom. Meals and breaks are not options. This I know for sure.

* * * * * * *

The nursing profession in the 1970s stood at the confluence of two important social phenomena: the emerging women's equal rights movement and expanding medical technology. As nurses shed their crisp uniforms and Dixie-cup-like hats in favor of white pantsuits and colored smocks, the disturbing image of the nurse as the doctor's handmaiden also seemed to be moving toward obsolescence. But as I soon learned, women still had a long way to go toward equality in the workplace.

The focus of nursing practice at this time remained on patient comfort, safety, and hygiene *à la* Florence Nightingale, but medical advances had begun adding layer upon layer of complexity to an ever-expanding job description. Overburdened and underpowered, nurses carried a load of patient care unheard of in American hospitals today. A registered nurse in a county hospital in the 1970's was expected to do the work of a number of medical specialists, serving as respiratory technician, pharmacist, phlebotomist, and diagnostician for as many as twenty-seven patients on a single shift. Few modern medical professionals can imagine this type of workload.

The change of shift report for our nursing staff was held in a large carpeted conference room by the central elevators. This spacious meeting place, sandwiched between the two hallways, was seldom used for any reason other than report. Most mornings I slid into a plastic chair at one of two card tables to begin writing the schedule for my team. My stomach tightened at the beginning of every shift as I began to see the work piling up. This was especially true if I'd been off for a couple of days. I'd just passed the licensing exam, and my position as team leader was pushing me to the limit. The patients on our unit suffered from a wide variety of ills– gunshot wounds, stabbings, major trauma, extensive burns, and radical cancer surgeries to name a few. Every shift brought new faces, new problems, and new challenges, and absorbing it all and mapping the day's activities was a skill in itself.

The paper schedule stood as a testimony to our horrendous work load. Empty beds on our post-op surgical floor were non-existent, and two teams, each consisting of one registered nurse (RN), one licensed practical nurse (LPN), and one nurse's aide, were responsible for the care of fifty-four patients. A single RN on night shift would often care for 54 patients with the help of aides. Sadly, this staff-to-patient ratio was a common occurrence in 1973. The entire hospital was chronically short-staffed, and it was no wonder. The ever-expanding role of the nurse, along with the less rapid development of social capital for women in the 1970s, resulted in draconian job expectations and low pay for nurses at County General and others hospitals like it. The starting wage for an RN at County was $3.90 per hour. Most RN's came to work at least an hour early. This extra time at the beginning of each shift was essential to get a handle on a day or evening or night, promising mayhem. Overtime pay was never offered.

The drill for report was always the same. RN's from the previous shift told their tales to the oncoming crew. They ran through the flip chart of cards detailing each patient's care plan as the new staff scribbled notes on a paper schedule. The grids of this schedule filled rapidly with each patient's name and the numerous things that needed to be done for every hour of the shift—patients to be turned, dressings to be changed, tube feedings, and respiratory treatments to be administered. Every patient would get a bath and oral care, and, if time, a back rub. It was the RN's job to give all medications, start IVs, draw blood after 8:00 a.m., change dressings, and monitor a diverse assortment of intravenous fluids, to include hyperalimentation and lipids, as well as help the aide and LPN get everything else done. There were no respiratory therapists or IV technicians to help, no pharmacists to mix the meds or IVs, and few, if any, machines to regulate the infusion rate of intravenous fluid.

As per routine, I posted the completed schedule on a door in the hallway. My team would refer to this resource frequently throughout the shift, crossing out treatments as they were done. Patient privacy wasn't an issue during this era. Records of temperature, blood pressure, intake, and output hung on clipboards at the foot of each bed for all to see to provide the rounding medical teams with the information they sought. There was no time for other charting. Unless something out of the ordinary happened (a death, an accident, or a massive infection), staff members seldom documented the care they did. No one had the time.

As happened on most mornings, the single night RN, Evelyn, lumbered in shortly after 7:00 a.m. and began her report of the night's happenings. Mr. Kramer developed a wound infection and was running a fever. Joan in Room 703 was transferred from ICU with a colostomy and would need a blood transfusion. The gun-shot wound in Room 722 pulled out his stomach tube, and it needed to be replaced. As per protocol, Evelyn went through the Kardex file that provided a brief synopsis of each patient's care plan, room by room, patient by patient. The on-coming staff took notes.

"The man in 706 was admitted at nine last evening," Evelyn stated wearily. Her skin had the pasty look of someone who works at night. Her head was covered with a blond nest of wild hair, and her uniform was stained with Betadine and coffee, both indicating of how hard she had worked. Her words came rapidly. She sighed a lot.

"The guy's a felon, charged with murder, chained to the bed with round-the-clock cops. They put in a chest tube at nine last night." She continued.

Evelyn went on to tell our team that a night shift aide found an eighteen inch metal trocar entwined in the felon's sheets, left in the bed by an intern who had inserted the tube into his chest during the evening shift.

"The patient never noticed the thing," Evelyn related with some awe, shaking her head and looking away. "The police guard sat outside the door unaware."

The intern's mistake could have meant disaster. The foot-long surgical instrument with a pointed end, used to break through the chest wall and guide the flexible plastic tube during its placement, could have been used as a lethal weapon. Report stopped for a moment as we discussed the awful possibilities.

"Two gunshot wounds were transferred out of ICU yesterday evening. A married couple shot each other arguing whether to have green beans or corn for supper." Evelyn rambled on, relating specific details of the couple's care and adding anecdotal tidbits here and there just to keep things interesting.

"The man in 709 was just admitted with a foreign body in his rectum." Evelyn stated without emotion. "He'll need a catheter." Notes flew onto the paper schedule. No one at the table blinked.

"The patient in 712 came in early this morning with lice.

He's had a shower and shave. I've never seen so many lice," Evelyn reported, her voice full of wonder. "We bagged his clothes, and I swear the plastic mass was moving. He's in liver failure and restrained. Story has it he was a nuclear physicist, but he blew his mind—alcoholic brain—Korsakoff's." My team listened in silence, trying to take it all in.

"Jim's still with us," Evelyn went on. "He's in the throes of a protracted death – on Dilaudid every three hours—last dose at six."

I winced at this news. We all knew Jim. He was a hero. I remembered the day he was first admitted to our floor for treatment of bone cancer. A blond, robustly handsome twenty-three year old wheeled onto the unit by his stunning girlfriend. Cancer had had its way reducing him to a grotesque skeletal figure languishing on a bed of suffering. The sight of his scalp, covered with outcroppings of bony lumps, broke my heart. All we had to offer, the strongest drug available in 1973, was a Dilaudid tablet dissolved in saline solution. These grainy injections, hitting bone, barely touched his pain. Every time I administered this shot I knew it wasn't enough.

Report continued, peppered with snippets of the dramas that never failed to play out on each and every watch. The staff frequently slipped into storytelling mode as a way to cope.

"Henry's asked us to call him Henrietta," Evelyn reported. "We've made an effort to comply." Henry was a transgender patient in for routine gallbladder surgery. His plans included a sex-reassignment operation sometime in the future after completing hormone therapy. He was a tall man with long, limp locks, a hint of a five o'clock shadow, and a barrel belly. His heavy pancake makeup and feminine jewelry, as well as his ultra-feminine persona, were strangely incongruous with his overall look.

We spent several minutes discussing the various feminizing treatments Henry would have to undergo before his gender reassignment surgery. Patients who'd undergone this procedure frequently passed through our ward for cosmetic surgery. We noted that most lacked the cellulite that plagued our female bodies. Henrietta's condition remained new to most of us. Although we tried, it was hard to understand.

Evelyn concluded our discussion. "Her name seems the least of her problems."

After the night nurse wrapped up her report, I routinely headed for my medication cart on wheels. Most of our patients were on intravenous antibiotics, and doses had to be reconstituted from powder. I began every shift by drawing up at least forty syringes of plain saline to get ready for the 9:00 a.m. run. Later, I squirted each ten cc syringe of sterile liquid into a vial of powdered antibiotic, shook it, drew the mixed medication back into the syringe, and marked each dose with a black china marker to indicate its contents before tossing it into the medication flip chart under the patient's name. I stopped this routine only to address immediate needs brought to my attention. The china marker was a must-have. I'd already learned that lesson.

Teams labored. Each patient was medicated, washed, toileted, and ambulated. Intravenous solutions were mixed, dressings changed. IVs checked and restarted, blood drawn, doctors' orders assimilated. The needs that arose on an average shift were many and unpredictable and often of the type that needed immediate attention. There were urinary catheters to be changed or checked, stomach tubes to be inserted or unclogged, burns to be treated, tracheotomies to be suctioned, bags and canisters to be emptied, IVs to start. Many of these tasks and procedures fell to the RN. Aides and LPNs on our floor didn't give medications, draw blood, insert tubes, or start and monitor IVs. Twenty-seven sick people relied on our meager team of three people to meet their needs.

As the team leader, I leaned heavily on my two co-workers, my sole and most excellent help. No blueprint existed for the number and variety of unwritten routines between the lines on the paper schedule. There was never a day when we weren't swamped, and because this load continued from day to day and never ended, it began to seem normal. Daily we trudged through our paper schedule, completing and crossing off an immense number of tasks, sometimes even volunteering for double shifts because an evening nurse called in sick. Some days I gave hundreds of medications and mixed more than twenty bottles of IV solution at the end of every shift to prepare for the next. I did this because I had to. Although most of us were under thirty (middle-aged nurses were a rare breed at County), every staff member went home mentally zapped and weary to the bone.

Of course, no one could plan for the inevitable crises that inevitably arose in the course of an ordinary day, interrupting our already overloaded schedule—the stuff of medicine that takes a person to the edge. Every shift brought its own set of problems.

Sometimes it was a new patient transferred from ICU with a list of complicated orders for every mode of treatment in the book, or a serial grouping of similarly encumbered, seriously ill individuals, with hoses in every orifice and imminent needs that overwhelmed. Sometimes it was an unaddressed issue that ignited to a crisis: an infection that went wild resulting in sepsis and shock; a feeding tube that became disconnected, dribbling a bag of Ensure to the floor; an IV that ran dry or infiltrated the tissues and had to be restarted. Sometimes it was negotiating with doctors as advocates for our patients. The workload kept most of us from focusing on our feelings. There was no time to pause and reflect or get philosophical. Every day had sufficient trouble of its own and sometimes that trouble hit broadside.

Chapter 8

Picking up the Pieces

It's 11:30 a.m. and Jorge Ruiz just pulled his call light. The ward clerk sitting behind the desk at the nurse's station pushes a button and speaks to him over the intercom. I'm standing by my med cart in front of the desk when she informs me that the patient is having pain. Jorge is two days post gallbladder surgery, and he's diabetic. I reach for the key to unlock the drawer of narcotics to get him a shot of Demerol. It's the tail end of the morning, and I am ready to give my noon meds. I have blood to draw, dressings to change, and several IVs to start. It's been a busy shift. What else is new?

As I draw the narcotic from a big bottle into a syringe, someone calls out that Jorge has stopped breathing. A code is called over the loud speakers. Every available staff member springs into action. I rush toward the alcove where the rickety metal crash cart of emergency medications is stowed, barrel down the hall and explode into the patient's room.

My staff is already up to speed, setting up oxygen and a balloon-like Ambu bag to breathe for Mr. Ruiz. Doctors in various stages of training have begun to descend on the scene, screaming questions about the patient's history and shouting instructions with voices full of authority. A nurse kneels on the bed to administer chest compressions. Her flowered underpants

49

can be seen through white pantyhose under the miniskirt of her uniform as she rocks and pumps on the patient's chest. No one seems to notice.

Interns and medical students continue to flood into the room, shouting instructions to inject glucose, Epinephrine, Lidocaine, and any number of drugs into the patient's IV tubing. Doctors insert a tube into Jorge's trachea, and an aide mans the flexible Ambu bag, squeezing it to deliver breaths of oxygen to the patient's lungs in a regular rhythm.

The flowered nurse continues to pump. Syringe wrappers and empty vials litter the floor beneath the cart. The flock of doctors is still barking orders, but with time there seems to be less urgency in their voices. The drugs aren't working. A few third-year medical newbies stand back, staring, arms folded in defense of their ignorance. They're not sure how to participate, and I sympathize. Up to this point, knowledge gleaned from hypothetical stories in textbooks has been their only reference, but this is real.

Our team continues to try everything in our bag of tricks—a long list of drugs, along with continuous cardiopulmonary resuscitation (CPR), but at some point it becomes evident that all efforts are failing. We can't get the patient's heart rate above 30 beats per minute. The tentative diagnosis: probable myocardial infarction (MI or heart attack) post-op cholecystectomy. The code is called. Mr. Ruiz is dead.

For a very brief moment no one speaks, and then doctors fly out of the room, scattering like a bag of marbles spilled on a tile floor. Aides stay to take care of the body and clear the debris generated by the code. They work together in efficient silence.

Soon Mr. Ruiz's body, covered in a sheet, is wheeled from the room and down the staff elevator to the morgue. Housekeeping swoops in. The room is tidied, the bed stripped, sanitized, and remade for the next occupant, who's waiting in the emergency room. Life goes on.

Science stands with ready answers to the "how "of death,

but its attempts to address the "why" always come up short. Why Mr. Ruiz? Why now? Why so young? Was it years of snacking on pork rinds in front of the TV, preventative medicine that slipped his mind, the exercise bike he never used, or the alcohol and cancer sticks he smoked that led to this tragic outcome after routine surgery?

If these explanations don't fit—because the patient is a young, non-smoking, non-drinking athlete and the picture of health—medical science punts to genetics, the mysteries of aging, or a confluence of known and unknown factors working to defy its logic: bad luck, bad karma, bad things happen. Scientific disciplines with their facade of control don't encourage deeper thought or look to find meaning in our short, troubled existence on the planet. They're into concrete facts and proven cause and effect. They seldom address the capricious nature of human tragedy.

As I leave Mr. Ruiz's room, Dr. Becker comes up to me in the hallway. He knows that Mr. Ruiz was under my care, and he offers a lifeline.

"Sometimes there's nothing you can do," he says looking down. "The guy had a massive MI."

Becker says his piece and walks away, but for an instant his eyes meet mine, and we see each other's pain. This is a golden moment. It's balm to my hurt. A verbal acknowledgement of the grief we share when a patient dies and a glancing recognition of our common humanity.

I'm overcome with this doctor's gift, so memorable because it's so rare.....so extremely rare. But I don't have time to let it sink in. Duty calls.

* * * * * * *

Later on that day, after finishing my meds, I decided to make a trip off the floor to transport a blood sample to the lab. Because of the extreme level of work required to keep things running on the ward, RN's rarely left the floor mid-shift, and I felt guilty abandoning my two co-workers. Mr. Ruiz's death earlier that morning left me drained, and I knew that even a short respite from the front lines would help. When the elevator opened I joined a group of housekeeping staff on their way to lunch. They were chatting merrily, trying to decide where to spend their golden hour away from the hospital.

"Let's go to Arby's," one man enjoined. Everyone seemed to agree.

High on caffeine and adrenaline, I wasn't really hungry, but the thought of a luxurious hour away from County General with lunch at Arby's suddenly sounded too good. As I overheard their banter, anticipating the fun, food, and freedom after a morning of cleaning up other people's messes, I felt an almost overwhelming urge to escape with them—to bust free, to have time to hear myself breathe, smell the newly-mown lawn in the park in front of the hospital, look up at the sky, and feel a cleansing breeze on my face. I wanted to be one of the tree-trimmers for the city, who made *more* than the $3.95 an hour that I was currently receiving for my services. I wanted to run away.

But leaving is never an option for a professional nurse. I returned to the floor after my errand to pick up where I left off. It didn't take long for me to fall into line. As the elevator doors opened and I stepped out onto the fourth floor, my nurse's aide ran up.

"A medical student took Mr. Jackson to X-ray and returned him to bed without his restraints. The confused patient pulled out his catheter, IVs, and rectal tube. There's urine, blood, and stool everywhere." she said with her head in her hands.

Someone had to deal with this mess. As usual, philosophic ruminations about life and death had to wait.

* * * * * * *

It was almost the end of my shift, and something wasn't right. My LPN accosted me in the hall to report that a patient in Room 712 was complaining of bedbugs. Although there was lots of work left to do before report, I took the news in stride, grabbed a few last-minute meds to give on my way, and hustled down the hall to investigate.

Clarence Carter, a six-foot six-inch tall black man, weighing close to three hundred and fifty pounds, was out of bed and headed for the door of his room as I entered. He was ranting about bugs, gesturing wildly with one hand and rolling an IV pole with the other. The glass IV bottle swayed and clanked on its metal stand, the plastic tubing whipped around his head and shoulders as he wobbled toward the exit. Three roommates, frozen in their beds, stared with wide eyes, cowering under their covers. Clarence's voice boomed as he bumbled toward me.

"Where's the manager?" he bleated, the back of his gown flapping open to reveal his doughy nakedness.

"Just a minute, Clarence, let's see what we can do here," I managed to say, trying to sound in control.

"What the _____? I've got to get out of this place!" he roared lumbering unsteadily toward the doorway to the hall, like a whirling dervish with an IV pole in tow.

I forced myself to stop for a second to take in the scene. My words belied the wild panic I felt. I was small and my only power lay in persuasion. There was no time to call for help.

I placed my hands with firm authority on Clarence's chest, and with steady weight guided him backwards, aiming for a heavy chair covered in blue plastic by the window between two beds.

"Sit down, Clarence," I managed to say calmly. "I'm going to get someone to take care of these problems."

To my relief, Clarence melted back with gentle pressure. He fell into the blue chair with a thud. I seized the bar at the side of the seat to snap the apron table across his lap.

Locked in like a toddler in a highchair, he stood stiffly,

lifting the heavy metal seat ever so slightly off the floor, trying to move like a hobbled Frankenstein. This was an impossible task that left him bellowing with frustration. Satisfied with his safety, I rushed into the hallway with my heart still pumping from an unwanted shot of adrenaline, and I glanced at my watch.

It was close to three o'clock, and although I still had IVs to mix and narcotics to count, I would soon be getting ready to go into report. Clarence exhibited all the signs of alcohol withdrawal–delirium tremens (DTs)–which was a condition that happened all too often with our patients. Classic symptoms included mental confusion, hallucinations, and tremors that required treatment with sedatives. The only available medications of this time were often under-effective, and four-point leather restraints were commonly used to keep the patient from hurting themselves and others. I'd have to get orders from the doctor to begin these interventions.

It was an unwritten law on our floor that staff attempt to take care of problems that erupted on their shift before transferring care. There'd be plenty of grousing by the nurses on evenings if they thought I hadn't tried. I grabbed an intern who happened to be walking by.

"Mr. Carter is going into DTs," I said, "Can we have orders?"

"Mr. Carter is going into DTs," the doctor repeated in his best rendition of a high-pitched voice.

"He's hallucinating." I pleaded.

The intern walked away smiling and didn't look back. He was mocking me.

Too tired to persist, I shot him a look of disbelief and headed to report. Evenings would have to deal with this situation. Although RNs worked on the front lines of responsibility on a floor rife with seriously sick and injured people, we often felt like a subservient underlings at the bottom of an invisible hierarchy. It was the worst kind of conundrum, and a theme repeated on a regular basis.

Minutes later I trundled into the conference room to share the news of the shift with my peers. No one was stunned to hear that a patient was beginning the DTs. No one was surprised that I'd averted a potentially catastrophic situation. No one was shocked to hear the doctor's response to my request for orders.

The next morning I learned that room 704 was closed for repairs. Sedatives and restraints were eventually prescribed during the evening shift, but not before Clarence threw a chair through the window of another patient's room. Before checking into report I walked down to see the damage. The room was freezing —air-conditioned from the outside. The table knife Clarence hurled at the charge nurse had left a hole in the wall by the door. I gazed at the hole and the shattered window imagining the scene that had transpired. Amazingly no one was hurt.

Shards of glass still covered the floor, and I reached for a nearby broom to sweep them up and dump them into the trash before heading to morning report.

Nurses are resilient, and learn to deal with whatever comes down. We pick up the pieces and move on. It was 1973 and just another day at County General. I was a professional nurse, and at age twenty-three that is what I did.

Chapter 9

Stuff and Go

It's about two p.m. on an ordinary day at County General, and I'm mixing IVs in the supply room when my aide Lucy asks me to talk to an uncooperative patient named Jack. I squirt a syringe of potassium into the bottle I'm working on and head to the room. I've known the patient for some time. He's a good-looking, dark-haired man of twenty-two, and he's dying of melanoma.

Lucy and I enter the room to find Jack slouched in a plastic chair by his bed with his back to us. He's wearing hospital-issue pajama pants and nothing else. He has an athletic build, and his broad back is covered with tiny dark moles. A bandage, stained with yellow drainage, covers his lower torso, and this is the problem. He's refusing to let the staff touch it.

"Hi, Jack. How about we change your dressing now and get it over with?" I say, all business. I stifle my feelings of impatience. I have *so* much to do and every second counts.

Jack doesn't move. He's turned away from us, shoulders hunched, head down.

My aide and I stare at his sullen form. We're both thinking about the next approach. What to do?

Troubling thoughts pulse through my mind: He's so angry. Who wouldn't be to have their life cut so short? Why did this have to happen? Why him? I imagine my boyfriend, Tom, in his place, acutely conscious of our good health and of the arbitrary nature of illness.

Choosing my words carefully, I select standard lines employed by medical professionals and parents throughout history to cajole balking people into accepting treatment regimes that hurt.

"Lucy needs to change your bandage, Jack. It will just take a minute. You'll feel so much better once it's done."

No response. Jack doesn't turn around.

I move on to the doctor card. "Your bandage is soaked, Jack. The doctor wants to keep it dry and clean. We don't want you to get an infection."

I can feel his rage, his silent brooding pocked with anger. He's going to die. Do we really expect him to care about a silly old dressing?

"Maybe you need something for pain," I offer with concern that I truly feel.

"Get out of here," he spits with venom, his back quivering, his body language communicating even more than his words.

Although it's rare, I've been in this place before. Sappy articles in nursing magazines expound on techniques to get uncooperative patients to toe the line—everything from pop psychology to bribery—but most nurses, like parents, have learned to pick their battles. Where there's anger, there's hurt. Although Jack's rage needed to be addressed, there are times when a person just needs some space.

"We'll come back in an hour, Jack, and see how you feel." I say. I make this offer hoping he'll appreciate our efforts to personalize his care.

Later that day Jack's hurt becomes a narrative in report: "He won't let anyone near. He won't listen. He's acting out." Jack's behavior makes our already hard job even harder, and the team feels justified in complaining. I understand the staff grumblings, but even so they bother me. Somehow I've caught a glimmer of where Jack is coming from and it's stopped me cold.

* * * * * * *

Some patients continue to surface on occasion like the plastic beach balls I tried to submerge in the pool as a child, only to have them shoot the moon. Images of certain people and situations pop up now and again like familiar friends. Jack was one such person. He passed through my life so briefly never knowing the impact his suffering had on me and my struggle with the meaning of it all.

Questions about the inscrutable nature of illness and tragedy hit every day during this period of my life, but they continued to be glossed over in the push to get the job done. I never spoke of them and neither did my co-workers. We realized that report wasn't the place to air our questions. Who had the time? Who had the answers? How would talking about these painful issues make things better? There was no place to go to stop Jack's kind of pain.

As a nurse I'd been trained to turn to science for solutions, but it didn't take long to discover medicine's limits and its often futile outcomes and common over-estimation of its power. Like a clipped telephone cable with a million disconnected multi-colored wires, a severed spinal cord would never again communicate with the brain. A comatose patient's state of consciousness frequently eluded all attempts to change it. Many diseases and genetic conditions had no cure. In an astounding number of situations, medicine offered only a modicum of comfort. Often it treated only the symptoms, tried a course of chemotherapy for metastatic disease, and maybe a little radiation, but couldn't cure the underlying pathology. Jack's stage of melanoma was and still is, almost always fatal.

It didn't take long for me to understand that science-based models of cause and effect were empty when it came to finding meaning. And even more importantly, limiting one's attention to objective information and excluding the subjective and less quantifiable aspects of life would sometimes lead to the wrong conclusions. I first realized this in my second year as a nurse at County General.

* * * * * * *

Helen was a sixty-nine-year-old woman with basal cell carcinoma. A sweet, average-looking grandma with the usual crisp gray hair and lined face of someone her age, she was admitted to County for surgical treatment of a growth under her left eye that looked like a brown mark on her cheek no bigger than a dime. An earlier biopsy had confirmed a slow-growing skin cancer called basal cell carcinoma that over time had tunneled its way through the tissues of her face. Doctors were planning a radical intervention. Helen made plans to meet with a surgical team, and she asked me to accompany her. Sadly, I rarely had time for this type of advocacy at County General, but I found myself drawn to Helen and agree to go with her to the conference. It must have been an unusually quiet day on the ward.

Since my very early days as a nursing student I'd been secretly plagued with skepticism about some medical interventions. During my training I saw surgical procedures that didn't improve the condition of patients, and I questioned the outcome of some radical treatments and operations in terms of the quality of life that the person was left with after submitting to them. Many patients underwent disfiguring head and neck surgery to "cure" their cancers only to die later after months of agony. I struggled to wrap my mind around the application of the Hippocratic Oath (first do no harm) as I imagine thousands have before me. This remains an age old problem: what to do when the so called "cure" is no cure at all and exponentially worse than the disease. The question of when to stop medical care, fraught with complicating factors and ethical dilemmas, remains an issue for doctors and their patients today.

Helen's planned surgery was extremely complicated and required the expertise of surgeons from a variety of disciplines. Experts in neurosurgery, plastic surgery, ear, nose, and throat, and several other specialties all convened in the report room to discuss her complicated treatment. The doctors sat at a long table at one end of the room. Helen and I faced them, feeling small, seated in two folding chairs at the center waiting for the team to speak. The doctors' excitement to tackle this complicated case oozed from their pores and permeated the room. Surgeons are always eager to do surgery, and this case seemed especially interesting. The chance to participate in a challenging operation was frequently seen as a coveted prize, especially for those eager to gain experience. I remember one doctor's inconsolable rage when a patient with terminal lung cancer refused to sign the consent papers to have one of his lungs removed.

Because the cancer had invaded one of Helen's eyes, the team's planned treatment included its removal. Helen wouldn't consent to this. As evidence of her lack of understanding about what the doctors were proposing, she agreed to the radical surgery with one condition: that her eye be spared.

Helen was old school and revered the doctors' authority. I advised her she that she could refuse the procedure. She didn't have to sign. I urged her to consider the plan and what it would mean. Because she refused to agree to having her left eye removed, she wouldn't be cured.

But one of the doctors told her that without surgery, as the basal cell spread, she would be unable to breathe and slowly smother. My own throat tightened when I heard this. I knew this wasn't right. This type of cancer grew very slowly and, at Helen's age, chances were that she would die of something else—heart attack, stroke, or simply old age. But the doctor's words had their desired impact. The prospect of suffocating to death scared Helen into submission. She signed the consent papers and was scheduled for radical procedure.

"The doctors know best," Helen assured me as we left the conference room. She grabbed my arm as we ambled back toward her room.

The next day Helen returned to our floor after twelve hours in surgery. When the bandages were removed, half of her face was gone. Hair that once grew on her head now grew from the space below her spared eye. Her scalp had been stretched to cover the wound. Her face had the look of a strange mutant—half human, half werewolf.

Weeks later, a nurse's aide wheeled Helen out of the hospital, her disfigured visage covered with a flowered scarf. We wondered about her future. Three months went by before the news came that she was dead. During her time at home, Helen never left her house again.

"If you cut, you're going to cry," goes an old adage for surgeons, alluding to the fact that surgery doesn't always go as planned. I knew this was true. But sometimes the plans for treatment were not so good.

I saw what happened to Helen. But I never cried.

Chapter 10

❧

Adrenaline Junkie

Exactly one year after that evening conversation in Pam's apartment at the nursing dorm, she asked me if I would like to meet her brother–the very same brother whose description left me so cold during one of our evening chat sessions. Pam's question and my answer would determine the direction of the rest of my life.

Tom and I met on a blind date in September of my second year of clinical training. By this time, I'd moved out of the nursing dorm to live closer to the main university. Several students carpooled from apartments off campus, and Pam and I wound up in the same car. Tom was just starting his freshman year fresh out of the army, studying pre-med under the GI bill. Pam thought we might jive.

My father once admonished me never to go out with a man who had a beard or a motorcycle; and my new beau had both. These traits alone were intriguing. Our first meeting proved exhilarating as Tom was smart and funny and cute. Days later, he bought me an extra- large motorcycle helmet, and we sped off together on his BMW, reveling in the speed and the beauty of undulating mountain roads around campus. As we stood in the parking lot of my apartment that afternoon and he adjusted the helmet on my extra-large noggin, I looked into his sky-blue eyes and felt the earth move.

But this blissful moment was just the beginning. Tom's parent's contentious divorce loomed in the background. Over the eight-year period that Tom and I dated, we broke up more times than I care to remember. A bouquet of roses arrived the morning after our first date, and with those flowers came a card on which Tom had written, "Have Patience." I put the card in the white leather Bible that my parents had given me for my confirmation. In the ensuing years of our on-again-off-again relationship, I would refer to it often.

The question of commitment stood at the center. Tom's pre-med studies consumed almost every waking hour and most days he was either attending classes, studying in the university library, or running track. During the early years of our courtship, he took a cross country trip by bicycle, ran several marathons, and spent one summer floating down the Yukon River on a raft, but marriage was one adventure he was unwilling to take. For most of my twenties, I found myself on an emotional roller coaster—either in the process of leaving Tom, reuniting with him, or unhappily separating to date others. The details of this period of my life, so full of angst and uncertainty, mark my first real experiences with personal grief.

One constant during this period was my job as a hospital nurse, which continued through my twenties. I often dreamed about leaving County and doing some other type of nursing outside the hospital setting *à la* the Cherry Ames stories I'd read as a kid, but I lacked direction or the gumption to make the change. For a few short periods, seeking a respite from the relentless stress at County, I tried the slower pace of nursing in private hospitals. Both moves came during a long and serious hiatus in my relationship with Tom, as I tried to reinvent my life and move on.

Moving away from County's massive work load failed to help my situation. Both private hospital positions left me unsatisfied. I told myself that I craved the creativity that County afforded, the power to invent solutions and address problems—a type of power that seemed unavailable in private hospital settings. But this was only partially true. Like a foreign correspondent on the front lines of a war, I'd become hooked on stress. Although it wasn't clear to me at the time, I was addicted to frenetic activity and high drama, which served as a powerful diversion from emotions I just didn't want to face.

As a nurse at private facilities, I was assigned two or three patients for "total patient care." Imagine the change after years of taking care of twenty-seven people on a huge surgical floor! Private hospital staffing rankled me. It seemed wildly inefficient and left me bored and unhappy. Patients in private facilities were typically less sick (few if any gunshot wounds and stabbings there), and patient care was often uncomplicated. I was used to medicating a large number of people from a heavy portable medication cart during shifts at County, so it seemed silly to be carrying a little tray with a couple of paper cups of pills for the few people under my care. At County, orders for pain meds were written with a range (i.e. Demerol 50-100 mg), and nurses determined the dose. At the private facilities there was no such freedom to make decisions in *any* area of nursing.

Accustomed to solving problems on my own, I frequently found myself in trouble for stepping out of rigid protocols. One day I applied a colostomy bag to a patient's wound drain to keep his skin dry and protected. I was sternly censored by an irate colostomy nurse who backed me into a broom closet to administer her scolding. Her frizzled gray hair seemed on springs as she shook her head in anger.

"You will call *me* and only *me* before you even think about putting a colostomy bag on a patient on this floor!" she screamed. "Is that understood?"

"But the patient doesn't have a colostomy" I protested.

"Nevertheless!" she shrieked.

I had no defense. Creative solution to an issue of patient well-being or not, I'd stepped into another nurse's territory.

This incident and others like it helped me to understand my place as a private hospital nurse. Authority trumped common sense. Some days at County I'd managed as many as forty intravenous lines, even more including hyperalimentation and intravenous lipids. I'd started IVs on almost every shift. In the private hospitals I was required to leave the care of IVs to the IV nurse. Even if a patient's IV slipped out of the vein and fluid had infiltrated the tissues making the patient uncomfortable, I was instructed to "let it be" and wait for the IV nurse to appear.

Numerous nursing decisions I'd made and procedures I did on rote at County now required doctors' orders. Something as simple as changing a dressing seemed to take a formal decree from a medical "pope." I felt overqualified and underutilized. Accustomed to being task-oriented, without tasks I felt adrift.

And there was another problem. Although I'd been trained to see the "whole patient" and treat each person's physical as well as emotional needs, the level of care that my job at County General demanded left no time for the softer side of nursing. The oppressive load of never-ending tasks that defined nursing practice at County prevented me from addressing the needs of patients who might require *more* than just another pill, procedure, or plan. It sapped reserves I might have used to deal with difficult patients like Jack, who struggled in the face of a dire prognosis. These types of situations surfaced every day. My troubled thoughts and feelings and those of my co-workers at County could easily be swept aside, buried in the business of the moment. In the quieter private hospital, with so much more time to focus, I found the emotional needs of my patients, especially relating to death, intensely uncomfortable.

One evening working on the floor of a private hospital, I was assigned to care for an elderly woman admitted to a regular patient room after a cerebral vascular accident (CVA). Earlier in the day she'd seemed healthy and full of life, but her massive stroke came without warning, damaging her brain and rendering her unresponsive and close to death. She was eighty-six.

The woman's frail and frantic husband of sixty years accosted me in the hall as I was leaving the supply room. His eyes danced with grief and wild words came choked with tears. His arms flailed as he approached. He came so close I thought he was going to hug me. I felt an immense drive to escape. Nothing I thought to say or do would make things better. I loved Tom, and I imagined what it would be liked being married all those years. I muttered some words of reassurance, but they felt empty and ineffective.

As the pain poured from this man, I felt it pour into me. It was a feeling I didn't like. It was too much like my earlier experience with Carrie and her paralysis; too much like what I felt at the hospital in Texas as I looked down on that comatose child. I had to get away.

No matter what the setting, my troubling feelings continued, but I wasn't ready to face them. I had a lot of questions, but no place to go for answers.

Chapter 11

❦

Edna

"Does it hurt?" The childish question had escaped Harry's lips before he could stop it. "Dying? Not at all," said Sirius. "Quicker and easier than falling asleep."

Harry Potter and the Deathly Hallows
by J.K. Rowling

Somewhere between the ages of nine and eleven, I had my first real encounter with human mortality. It came early in my career as a Girl Scout when the leader of our Brownie troop encouraged us to volunteer at a local nursing home on Saturday mornings. As part of our Community Service badge, my Brownie friends and I were assigned to play games and provide some youthful cheer to elderly residents at a rest home in Bellerose. My healthy grandparents and Dad's robust aunts and uncles had been my only exposure to older people to date. As I remember, the reality of ailing old age came as quite a jolt.

Girl Scouting provided loads of wonderful friendships, stretched my horizons, and enriched my world beyond the confines of my supremely sheltered home life. Some of my best memories from childhood are the summers I spent at Blue Bay

Girl Scout Camp in the Hamptons, trips to the city with our troop, and laughing with friends at weekly meetings as we worked to earn badges.

Our leader, Mrs. Cohen, stood out as a remarkable woman who concentrated her efforts on providing the girls in her charge with all the important experiences of childhood. Wearing rumpled slacks, coke-bottle glasses, and deodorant that failed to cover, she labored on to show the young ingenues in our troop the world.

I can still see Mrs. Cohen's crown of wild hair flying as she tried to shuffle a flock of unruly ten-year-old girls through the subway in Manhattan. Barely five feet tall, she wedged her tiny body between the closing doors of the subway car until each girl made it through. She taught by example at every meeting and showed us that, as girls, we possessed the power to shape our own experience of life. She proved a paragon of courage, who encouraged us to embrace all that the world had to offer.

I remained wild about Girl Scouting well into my teens. I wore my sash with its gold pins and machine-embroidered circles with pride. Chef, Folk Dancer, Lifesaver, and the like—every badge marked a milestone. Due to Mrs. Cohen's diligence, most of the girls in our troop went on to achieve the highly coveted Curved Bar Award—the female version of the Boy Scout Eagle Rank in the 1960s. My sonless parents made a big deal of this event, and the big award ceremony that followed, but most of the girls in my troop were chagrined at all the fanfare. Scouting was fun. The hard work everyone was applauding simply didn't register.

The cheap metal clasp of the Curved Bar Award broke off as I fondled my prize on our way home in the car, so the pin never made it to my sash. But the memories live on. Mrs. Cohen inspired her scouts to reach for the stars. I remain forever grateful for that.

My assignment for that Saturday morning project at the nursing home so many years ago was a ninety-year-old woman named Edna. Pale, frail, and dressed in a faded flannel gown, she sat folded over in a wheelchair in the great room by the foyer looking sad. I stood by her chair feeling stupid—a skinny eight-year-old in a Brownie uniform and felt beanie, quaking with anxiety. We stared at each other at first, not sure how to proceed. As I recall, the time we spent together seemed okay. We played checkers. I was willing to go back.

But when I returned to the facility the following Saturday and went down the hall to Edna's room, she wasn't there. Her dingy living space with its dull linoleum floors and sagging Venetian blinds had been stripped bare of the ephemera of life and reverberated with emptiness. I stood for some time in the hallway outside her room waiting for instructions. I lingered in that doorway staring at her lonely hospital bed with its bare metal frame and glossy gray plastic mattress. A nurse came by to tell me that my new friend had passed away. At the age of eight I was just beginning to realize what that meant. Edna was gone. She wouldn't be back.

And that was it for me and the nursing home, at least for several decades. Community service would have to happen someplace else. So began a long, uneasy relationship with death.

As a nurse I met death regularly. Almost always unwelcome, its countless variations-on-a-theme routinely left the medical staff scrambling to hold it at bay. Young or old, expected or unexpected, only the sorrow stayed the same. Each death so final. Each one a sad goodbye.

It would take many years before I would come to any kind of peace with mortality. The problem of pain included death, and its inscrutable, inequitable nature continued to gnaw at me well into my forties. As grandparents, parents, and friends died, each experience reopened old questions about meaning and unfairness. No explanations satisfied.

I went on to spend many years stuffing it all, putting everything into storage, where it stayed unaddressed. Through college, my time as a hospital nurse, and into my forties I seemed to go about my business unaffected by what I faced. But single snapshots of scenes and experiences remained recorded on an imagined videotape in my mind. I took on baggage.

It would be years before I unpacked these memories for a closer look, years before I actively sought to address issues simmering beneath the surface. The usual place to go for this kind of reflection seemed unavailable to me. The church and I had history.

Chapter 12

Limbo

The year is 1963, and I'm thirteen years old. It's ten minutes before five, and my stomach's growling for dinner. Stifling a squirm, I sit motionless in a pew at St. James Lutheran Church in Stewart Manor, New York, counting the seconds until I can bust loose and pedal home through the tree-lined streets of Floral Park on my Schwinn. My peers and I have been sitting for close to two hours in the stuffy church, and we're all ready to blow. We're dutiful children and we've been submitting to one of the rites of passage common to our era. In accordance with a fashionable unwritten code for good parenting in the early1960's, we've been sentenced to two years of religious instruction better known as weekly catechism class.

The sanctuary of St. James is dimly lit and smells of must and cedar. Pastor Dietrich, dressed in a dark tunic with a high white collar, stands at a lectern by the altar, gesturing with a closed Bible. His voice thunders with characteristic zeal. He's admonishing his adolescent charges to avoid the inadvertent use of a conversational "gee," which might be short for "Jesus," and castigating us teenagers for our earlier unregenerate language. His acerbic words, sodden with reproach, wash over the children in his captive audience, baptizing them with fear. We cringe as he describes hell and warns of the perils of angering God. His invective ends with specific instructions on the proper way to take communion.

"The altar is not a soda fountain or a cocktail bar!" he screams. "Guzzling is not allowed!" His deep voice booms off the rafters of the almost empty room. Sullen, we listen, taking it all in.

Many months later, dressed in long, white satin robes and red beanies, our class walks single file down the center aisle of the church on a Sunday morning. The sanctuary's packed with families who've come to observe us take our first holy communion. It's a big event. Many relatives have come to witness our dedication. My mother's planned a party.

I'm not sure how my classmates feel, but I don't understand all the fuss. The meaning of the communion ceremony doesn't register. I approach the altar full of trepidation, afraid to tip my head back too far as I drink the so-called "fruit of the vine" lest God interpret my movements as an irreverent swig and be sorely displeased. This remains my only thought as I partake of the sacrament. The pastor's words reverberate, seared into my psyche. "No guzzling!" I will never receive communion again without hearing them.

* * * * * * *

There was nothing spiritual about my experience of catechism class as a young teen, nothing to lift my thoughts beyond myself and my tight little world of teenage angst and activity. This religion smacked of the "step on a crack and you'll break your mother's back" superstition. God loomed as a vengeful punisher, so you'd better be good. Prayers were like letters to Santa, the Bible a storybook with dated, unbelievable, and violent stories. Church was just something our family did on Easter, Christmas, and once in a while on a Sundays. Matching shoes, hat, and handbag in place, I vegged out in the pews on these occasions, more aware of the pinching of my new garter belt than of the presence of a Higher Power.

In 1968, like so many of my generation, I headed to college relishing my escape from the confines of catechism dogma to strike out on my own. The year was 1968. The times were a-chang'in. A generation experimenting with options, defining its own truth, had begun to test the solid rules that were offered by parents and the church in such a neat package. Of course, few serious issues had come up in my own life at this point, but I was bursting with youthful hubris, suspicious of easy truth, and confident I'd find my own way.

The horizon teemed with choices. In a culture applauding individuality, diversity, and the freedom to choose, the world offered a rich salad bar of beliefs that could be personally designed to suit each diner's tastes. The church of Pastor Dietrich, with its rigid laws and proclamations, seemed to be based on fuzzy myths that stifled my restless spirit. I left for college, glad to leave the stuffy religion of my childhood behind.

Although Bible knowledge gleaned from my early religious training would later serve to bewilder friends and acquaintances, I considered its content meaningless—empty factoids perpetuated by constant repetition and sanctimonious self-deception. When I won a Bible trivia contest at a gathering of collegiate friends, the unusual combo of my wide knowledge of scripture and blasphemous rejection of its message left some church-goers slack-jawed and speechless. All the doctrinal material so solidly hammered into my impressionable mind during the years of catechism remained, but relevance was lacking.

At that time in my young life, I judged Christianity by Christians, and I didn't like what I saw. In fact, I eventually came to see Christianity as a mere step-up from the image of the beaming, glassy-eyed Hare Krishnas peddling flowers in the airport.

An acquaintance in college fell in with the Krishnas. I don't remember much about her except that she was chubby (over two hundred and fifty pounds) and had a great sense of humor. I do recall the day a friend and I went to visit her at her new apartment. We hadn't seen her for some time, and we were concerned.

Linda answered the door dressed in a long robe that appeared to be made out of a white bed sheet. Similarly clad people could be seen milling around behind her in the apartment. She stood in the doorway with the door cracked to speak to us. She wouldn't let us in. Her normally fleshy face appeared gaunt, and, despite her loose robe, it was obvious that she'd lost more than half of her body weight. There was something wrong with her eyes. She looked beyond us, both orbs glazed as if in a trance. Her words were devoid of inflection. Linda told us she'd sold everything she owned to follow her faith. The old Linda was gone. This incident made an impression. *This is what religion could do.*

My college roommate found comfort in a charismatic church and often told me she was praying for me. Her words irritated. One day her pastor showed up at the apartment to talk to me about conversion to Christianity. I listened to his diatribe with a critical ear and offered what I perceived to be smart and respectful answers to counter all of his points. His parting words were memorable only because of the pride I felt. "You're the hardest nut I've ever had to crack!"

Christians seemed disingenuous: smiling phonies, every one. The rhetoric flowing from their pulpits turned me off. I reeled at the blatant hypocrisy of a religion that ardently opposed the killing of the unborn but supported the bombing, murder, and maiming of men, women, and children who had *already* been born. I bristled at a church that seemed to be the right arm of the culture of greed and materialism, smug in the salvation of its members, unable to examine its cultural complicity or to see beyond a narrow worldview that it defended with pugnacious rancor.

Though troubling questions continued to bubble to the surface now and again, I put them all on a back burner. Throughout my early adult years I lived in a sort of spiritual no-man's land. In fact, I lived in this limbo well into my forties. I didn't claim to be an atheist.

I just didn't claim anything.

Chapter 13

Trapped

We never touch people so lightly
that we do not leave a trace.

Peggy Tabor Millin

It is a typical day shift at County General in late 1978, and, armed with information from report, I head down the hall to evaluate the patients under my care. I enter the room of a young woman and part the curtains around the bed to look in. The patient is twenty-seven years old and morbidly obese. I was told by night staff that she was weighed on a freight elevator on her way to the hospital and that she tipped the scales at close to six hundred pounds.

Cindy is scheduled to have this surgery today, and I will be giving her a pre-op injection. I walk to the head of her bed. Short dark hair frames her face, but the rest of her features are nondescript, disappearing in puffy folds of fat that fall from her chin like layers of thick pancakes. She's lying on her side with her eyes closed. Two beds have been pushed together to accommodate her bulky frame.

"Cindy, I'm your nurse today. How are you doing?" I ask.

Her eyes are closed and she doesn't answer. I sense she's feigning sleep. I touch her on the shoulder, but she doesn't move. A single paper-thin sheet hides her nakedness. No hospital gown is ample enough to cover her massive form. I look down in silence. I feel her humiliation as I lift the drape to reveal the body of her own creation—her shame. I sense her anger toward herself, at what she's done to wind up in this place. I feel her rage as doctors and medical students and nursing staff, her peers in age, come into the room and expose her private anguish, laying it bare.

* * * * * * *

Cindy had been admitted to undergo a jejunoileal bypass—a type of surgery invented in the 1950's as a treatment for extreme obesity. This procedure, which is no longer done today, involved looping off all but a twelve to eighteen-inch loop of the normally twenty-feet-long small intestine to prevent the absorption of calories. This surgery frequently produced a number of distressing complications that included mineral and electrolyte imbalances, protein malnutrition, and arthritic-dermatitis, all later thought to be caused by bacterial overgrowth in the excluded blind loop of small intestine. As a nurse at County, I frequently witnessed jejunolileal bypass patients returning for mandatory surgical reversal of the procedure. They came back to the hospital cachectic—shriveled images of their former selves suffering from severe chronic diarrhea and a host of other serious problems including liver failure. Even those who had a relatively benign course remained at risk for liver disease later in life. This dangerous procedure was still being done in the early 70's.

After passing out my morning meds, I went back to Cindy's room. Her eyes remained closed, and she appeared to still be sleeping. I continued to talk to her but my questions remained unanswered.

My mind leaped forward to issues of her care. Her

cumbersome body remained inert as I lifted one of the heavy rolls of flesh that cascaded in tiers from her torso with both my hands to expose excoriated skin underneath. How would we manage her skin after surgery? How would we turn her? Her post-operative care seemed daunting.

I thought about a story I'd heard in report recounting her conversation with a medical student the previous day.

"She told him she only eats one egg and a piece of toast for breakfast," the night nurse chortled. "And skips dinner!"

We laughed at the absurdity of it all—the silly diet history and Cindy's creative response. I identified with Cindy. I too might amuse myself by toying with an earnest but clueless medical student on a misguided mission.

"She must be a light eater," an aide offered. "She eats non-stop, but only while its light."

More chuckles ensued. But under our laughter, real sadness percolated. Frequent attempts to create humor in the face of patient calamities were just ways to handle frustration. The city's "knife and gun club," regularly filling our surgical floor with stabbing and gunshot victims, continued its regular meetings. Violence, habitually resulting from the abuse of the *sad trio* of sex, alcohol, and drugs, served as one constant in most of the tragedies we saw. The devastating consequences of dysfunctional human behavior poured down in unrelenting torrents as if from an incontinent sky with no end in sight. Numerous inane variations on a theme just kept on coming, and they no longer held the power to surprise.

"It's time for your pre-op shot, Cindy," I said later in the morning. But Cindy didn't acknowledge my presence.

I administered the injection, gently replaced her covers, and headed out of the room to deal with the never-ending list of duties calling for my attention.

Cindy would never know it, but many years later I would remember our meeting as an epiphany that exposed a certain truth. I'd missed the mark. I'd failed. We're all brothers and sisters on this planet full of pain. Feeling and taking the time to act on this heart knowledge would always be essential to good nursing care.

Perhaps I could have let Cindy know that I sensed her suffering and remorse and shared some of my own regrets over bad choices I'd made. Perhaps I could have revealed the prickling anger percolating under my cool facade as I stifled my feelings on every front. Perhaps I could have told her that I too felt trapped—mired under the weight of an impossible job, rejected and unable to move past a seven-year relationship with a boyfriend who refused to get married, literally over-stuffed with unexpressed emotions assaulting me from many directions. Perhaps we could have laughed together about the medical establishment's senseless compulsion to collect objective data at the expense of the expression of human compassion. Perhaps we could have been friends.

But on that day in 1978 this was not to be. Cindy and I would never know each other beyond the superficial stereotypes we'd perceived on that day—a too-busy nurse with crazy responsibilities and her morbidly obese patient headed for surgery.

My practical concerns about Cindy's physical care were soon moot. Later that day we received word: She died on the operating table.

Chapter 14

❦

Burned

It's the early afternoon on an ordinary day in 1979, and I am barely holding on. It's been over six years since I graduated from nursing school, and I'm back at County General. Although I'm young and used to the rigors of day-shift nursing, my legs ache and I'm frazzled. I've been buzzing on coffee since 6:00 a.m. and feel toxic. Requests for my attention pour from every direction, and all mental circuits are beginning to shut down, close to fried. The events of this particular day on the ward have been building.

As usual, the entire hospital is grossly understaffed. As a way to compensate for a shortage of nurses in intensive care, the unit has been periodically moving desperately sick patients to the floor. Our skeleton crew is already stretched thin with two RNs caring for fifty-four people. How much more can we take?

Our new head nurse demonstrates a hands-off management style. She's young and inexperienced and spends most of her day in meetings or ensconced in an office behind the break room. It's a tiny cubicle cluttered with paper documents and stacks of policy manuals and little else. On a good day, she offers a passing nod to the peons who labor with the sick, sans leadership, before disappearing into her papered haven. On a bad day, she's off the floor by 8:00 a.m. slipping quietly into the elevator, standard clipboard in hand, on her way to destinations unknown. In the rare instance we catch her long enough to verbalize our concerns, she puts us off, backing away while we talk, looking past us as she expresses empty empathy with a terse demeanor and wandering eyes. Nothing changes.

The head nurse is gone as usual when the news arrives that ICU will be transferring patients on respirators to the floor. These are very sick people. They can't breathe on their own. The unthinkable is happening.

My RN cohort, a petite forty-something strawberry blonde named Ann, is the best of the best, and she looks frantic. We stand by the nursing desk and watch as the ICU staff wheels two patients, their respirators, and assorted machines with paraphernalia down the hallway on one side of the unit. Our panic is visceral. Normally, as team leaders, we work in tandem, but in a rare showing of comradeship, our eyes meet to share mutual dismay. Can they really do this?

* * * * * * *

These horrendous working conditions were the norm at County General in the 70's. Somehow we coped. But at least for me, a change was coming. On one day in 1979, a single painful incident became a spark that ignited something that eventually set me free.

As things progressed on that particular day, the demands of an already impossible job were beginning to escalate to the point of insanity. Respirator patients with tracheotomies needed suctioning. Numerous IVs, often dependent on arm position to maintain any consistent of infusion, were either running way behind or running dry, and new orders from doctors were backing up. The patient in room 726 had been incontinent with diarrhea needed help and the smell wafted out into the hallway. Patients called for pain medications, and an aide reported that a patient's urinary catheter had sprung a leak. To top it off, I still hadn't given all the noon meds. Pulled in a number of directions, I could feel my hold on things slipping as I desperately tried to get organized.

I was standing on weary legs, mixing a new bottle of IV solution on the portable med cart in the hallway by the elevators when I looked up to see a third-year medical student headed my way. His gait was stiff, and he looked all business. He was carrying a patient's chart. *Now what?*

"I want to talk to you about Mr. Jackson's care," the student mumbled, fumbling to open the chart. I suppressed the urge to roll my eyes. *Just what I needed.* An overwhelming desire to ignore him and walk away swept over me.

It had been months since the patient in question had been admitted through the ER with a gunshot wound to his spleen, and he was well-known by our staff. After surgery and life-saving blood transfusions, he had developed a rare condition marked by pronounced, constant, uncontrollable body movement. After nearly two months in ICU, doctors moved him to our post-op floor with his jaws wired shut to prevent damage to his teeth from the constant spasms. Liquid meals administered through a tube inserted directly into the patient's stomach provided his daily nutrition, but the doctors wanted him to start eating. For days we'd been trying to get him to take blenderized food by mouth. Mr. Jackson would have none of it.

"Has Mr. Jackson been getting his 30 cc's of liquid food by mouth every twenty minutes as ordered?" the medical student inquired. His owlish eyes looked out from under bushy eyebrows, and sweat glistened on his forehead. He was a plebe, direct from college classroom central, just beginning his clinical work. There was hint of authority in his tone. He was trying to play doctor.

I stared at him in disbelief. I'd been in Mr. Jackson's room to administer his noon tube feeding. I'd seen the rows of cups containing puréed mystery meat, vegetable paste, and pulverized fruit, all left over from previous shifts, rotting in Styrofoam on every available flat surface by the bed. The patient hadn't touched a drop of the mushy pulp. Not knowing how long the stacks of unrefrigerated mash had been sitting in the stuffy room, I swept the whole mess into the garbage and called it good. *A new tray with the same pureed offerings would come with the next meal. That would have to do.*

My response to the med student was hard and unkind.

"Dr. Judd, I don't have time for this. A tray of puréed food has been delivered to Mr. Jackson's room at every meal. Cups of food paste have been piling up for days, and he won't touch it. If you want him to have his pap, then you'll have to go in there and offer it yourself." Rage of volcanic proportions bubbled up in me. Usually slow to anger, my strong reaction to this naive student surprised even me.

The addled med student began to argue, but I wouldn't participate. I couldn't get away from him fast enough. With so many patient needs pressing, his very presence felt like a needle in the brain.

"I can't take this!" I snapped. "Get out of my sight." I left my cart and ran down the hallway ducking into a patient room to check the catheter. The act of moving quickly dissipated some of the emotion. I didn't look back.

Minutes later I was once again standing by the cart labeling bottles of IV fluid when I looked up to see a third-year resident marching toward me. The intensity of his movements telegraphed that he was on a mission, and fuming. It was obvious that the medical student had reported my frank insubordination, and this resident was coming to give me my due. I barely had time to brace myself for his onslaught.

"You idiot!" he screamed in a voice that seems to rattle the vials of saline and bottles of IV fluid on my overloaded cart. "You slacker! Your attitude stinks! I mean *stinks*! I have never seen worse!"

A few people gathered to listen sympathetically as he rattled on. This doctor had a reputation. He had berated staff in the past, blowing into change of shift reports to complain of our staff's general incompetence, spewing expletives and acid anger. But never had his venom been so personal.

Although I saw his red face and his wild arms gesturing with wrath, chopping the air as if he wanted to decapitate me, his words didn't register. I acted deaf and numb and felt strangely disconnected from the whole ugly scene. When he'd finished his screed, I retreated to the med room behind the nurses' desk to collect my thoughts. A few women surrounded me to offer sincere consolation.

As usual our head nurse was nowhere to be found. A trip to nursing administration to discuss this incident would prove non-productive. My meager social capital wouldn't cover the cost of my insubordination. I had no recourse. The medical hierarchy reigned supreme.

Patients continued to call. There was no excuse good enough to warrant abandoning them or my team. Thoughts of walking away were pushed aside as I slipped back into a role that was far too familiar. Despite my anger I soldiered on. Pressed to deal with an unpleasant situation, I summoned "Granite Janet" into service. I knew that she was able to stuff and go.

I completed the shift. I returned to work over the weeks that followed as if nothing happened. But something *did* happen. Burnout, defined as fatigue, frustration, and failure to invest resulting from prolonged overwork, stress, and intense activity, had become all too real. I knew my days as a hospital nurse were numbered.

Soon the years-long conflict over marriage that so painfully consumed my twenties would resolve. Soon I would return to County General only in the darkness of my anxious dreams. Although it would take over thirty years, the long, slow slide out of nursing, which was supposed to be my life's profession, had begun.

Months after the incident with the irate and clueless resident, when I finally quit County General for good, I remember looking back at the front door as I made my final exit. So many people had passed through my life during those years. I'd seen so much heartache and suffering. On that day I was twenty-nine but felt so tired and old.

My soul felt heavy as I walked through the parking lot. For that one brief moment I was overcome with a very acute sense of the load I had been bearing, and how it had changed me. It would be some time before I realized just how much.

Chapter 15

Suffering Comes Home

In the summer of 1979, Tom and I were finally married under a canopy of trees in his mother's backyard. Everything changed one Tuesday evening when Tom called to let me know that Hans, his elderly dog, had died. I was out on a date at the time with a man who was most definitely not a love interest, but my roommate was not savvy to the status of my current relationship. She told Tom that I was with my boyfriend. After all those years of struggle a little triangulation was all it took.

The day of our wedding was cool and clear, and the sky shimmered with blueness, providing the perfect backdrop for our happiness. The bridesmaids and a few of the wedding guests cried as we recited our vows—touched by a marriage that had been so long in coming. When my brother-in-law dropped a noose from the trees overhead and the groomsmen crooned the old Western tune "The Hanging Tree," all tears turned to laughter in a burst of comic relief. Our long courtship had been hard on everyone. After eight years of living with our vacillating relationship, the solemn ceremony and the humor that followed proved cathartic. The years of painful uncertainty were behind.

For the first part of our marriage, Tom and I lived in a split-level house in a suburb of a city affectionately known as the "armpit" of the state—a working-man's town on the interstate, dominated by a huge steel mill. Tom was completing his family practice residency. Our house near the hospital was comfortable but needed work so we spent our weekends painting, papering, and generally sprucing up the place to make it a home.

Marriage brought few surprises. We had, after all, gone through a lot together over the last eight years. Most of our married friends from medical school had already produced several children. With a group of ready-made residency friends and lots of old ones from college, we settled into life like the old married couple we'd emulated for so long.

Tom spent long hours at the hospital during the week and moonlighted at rural emergency rooms on weekends, so it wasn't long before I felt the call to go back to work. After spending a few weeks acclimating to my wifely role in the home, I started looking for a job. Still smarting from fresh burnout wounds, I briefly consider another career path, but, in the end, a part-time position working in medicine seemed a natural solution. With a bachelor's degree in nursing, what else would I do?

At the beginning of this adventure I attempted a few shifts at a local private hospital, only to revisit the same blistering boredom and crippling claustrophobia I'd experienced at other private facilities as a puppet nurse, sapped of responsibility and hamstrung by the rules. I marveled at staffing levels that assigned one RN to two patients and at the poor quality of care that people received. Nurses were often unable to come up with answers to even the most basic questions about their patients' diagnoses and care.

One specific scene pops to mind when I think of this private hospital experience. I was sitting at the nursing station on a surgical floor of a private hospital waiting to be briefed about one of the two patients I would be caring for:

"What's wrong with Mr. Casey?" I asked, genuinely hoping for accurate information.

The charge nurse looked uneasy. "He's here to be medicated,"

Feeling testy, I continued to badger her. "What's he being treated for? What's his problem?"

"I'm really not sure," the nurse grumbled looking uncomfortable. "He's on several medications."

"What medications?" I continued, indignation rising in my throat.

"You'll have to look in the Kardex."

What a change from the detailed, hour-long reports at County General! Nurses at this particular private hospital seem like uniformed babysitters with pill-pushing privileges. Full of self-righteous arrogance, I felt justified in my outrage. Shift to shift it was always the same sloppy care; my irritation continued to build. To address this raging discontent, just as I did in nursing school, I decide to up the challenge and accepted an assignment to intensive care. I should have known better.

It was ten thirty p.m. when dressed in a short polyester uniform and white rubber-soled Oxfords I reported for duty at the personnel office of a small private hospital in our home town. An assignment was posted on a bulletin board by the door, and I grabbed it on the way to the elevators. My official title was float nurse, and I'd be filling in for the night-shift RN in the surgical intensive care unit (ICU). I headed upstairs to get a tour of the unfamiliar facility and be briefed by the evening nurses. Much to my surprise, I found out that I'd be working *alone*. Red flags flew. One of the RNs reassured me.

"Don't worry," she offered. "We only have two patients, and they're both doing well. You'll be fine."

Although I was used to taking care of a large number of seriously sick people, ICU wasn't my area of expertise. I looked out over the large room. The two patients on respirators seem to be sleeping. Four beds were empty. *Two patients? How bad could it be?*

After my tour and a brief report that was better than most, I jumped to the tasks that had become so familiar. I took the patient's vital signs, listened to their lungs, adjusted IVs, and checked tubes for patency. I measured input and output and administered medications and treatments on schedule. I checked respirator settings and oxygen levels. Both of my charges were suctioned and turned. Everything seemed fine. I settled in for a night of routine activities. I was floating.

But around three thirty a.m. the phone rang. The recovery room nurse was calling to tell me she'd be transferring a post-surgical patient to my unit. The patient's emergency surgery revealed an abdomen full of inoperable cancer. This was a terminal diagnosis euphemistically termed "an open-and-shut case."

Before the advent of modern diagnostic tools (MRIs, CAT scans, and the like), many people underwent surgery without a clear picture of what was causing their problems. In such situations, the inside of the body cavity would be packed solid with petrified cancerous tumors encircling and crowding internal organs compromising their function. Upon discovery of this type of pathology, the surgeon would close the incision and send the patient back to the floor with instructions to get their affairs in order. Despite this sad prognosis, most patients returned home and had time to do just that. But some were not so lucky. That night in the ICU my new patient began the process of dying minutes after being transferred.

The recovery room nurse helped me transfer the unconscious man from the gurney to the bed. I took his vital signs, dismayed to find his blood pressure low and his heart rate high—a bad combination. I called the surgeon.

The patient's doctor ordered a series of standard measures by phone—a host of intravenous drugs requiring careful administration and constant monitoring. If only I'd had a clue about protocol and about where the medications and equipment were stored. This was my first time in this hospital, and it had been some time since I'd administered these types of medicines. Frantically I searched for the equipment and vials I needed. Unfamiliar drugs and dosages that required calibration swamped my brain. (Today syringes often come pre-filled, but in the 70's we routinely mixed and measured our own medicines.) Our nursing curriculum failed to include even the simplest math course. I scrambled to calibrate each dose using the rusty algebra I learned in high school.

My mind labored to prioritize as I dashed from one patient to the next. If only I had an aide or another staff member to watch the two other sick patients who needed my attention. I phoned the supervisor but help never came. The drugs weren't working and the new patient's vital signs were deteriorating.

I continued to call the doctor as the man hovered between life and death. Orders kept coming and I did my best to follow them. Somehow I was able to care for all three people and to suppress the overwhelming panic barely held at bay. Thankfully, the sick man clung to life. Four hours later, sweating from exertion and stress, and trembling with emotion, I turn the care of the three critically-ill people over to the day staff. At that moment, everyone was still alive. Memories of my time at County General still burned, and this ICU trauma opened old wounds.

* * * * * * *

Shortly after the private hospital ordeal, a temporary job as a visiting home health nurse at the county health department became open. The RN in charge of a section of the county was taking sick leave. I jumped to apply. A position helping patients to recover in their own homes, past needing acute care, promised to afford me ways to be creative in unique environments. I'd have the freedom to make decisions and my own schedule. It seemed too good to be true.

On my first day as a home health nurse, I visited a woman with an infected wound who lived with her sister in a quaint Craftsman style home in an established part of town. The house smelled of mothballs and chicken soup and was decorated with the ceramic knickknacks and froufrou one might expect in the home of two elderly women: doilies on the arms of overstuffed chairs, lace curtains, and needlepoint pillows. The home was airy and light. The sisters were chatty and fun and craved my attention.

The younger sister was a recent widow recovering from hip surgery. The older one had never married.

"I'm the healthy one," the older sister bragged, with merriment in her eyes. "Marriage takes its toll."

I listened to their stories of days long past and had the time to laugh at their jokes. I washed the patient's wound and change her dressings, reveling in our easy relationship and the chance to be a little creative with her care. I looked forward to seeing the sisters every morning. I felt as if I'd found my niche.

But within days I realized that home health would not always be that easy. Because patients were in their own homes, I faced situations and environments that often left much to be desired. Many families struggled to care for helpless loved ones without adequate help and people of all ages were sometimes trapped in their beds by illness and disability with no end in sight.

I soon learned that the houses and the patients who lived in them were as different as their diagnoses. The beautiful mansion with a baby grand piano and panoramic view housed an elderly woman in a rented hospital bed dying of colon cancer in a back bedroom. The nondescript bungalow in a row of clones was home to a heart attack victim waiting for his daughter to come home after the night shift to lift him into his wheelchair. The brand new condominium sheltered a comatose teenager. The tiny one-bedroom apartment in a high-rise building served as a haven for an elderly grandmother in a vegetative state after a devastating stroke. Even that little shack behind the garage without running water provided a simple one-room shelter for a frail octogenarian who was spending her last days on her couch alone without even a radio or television for company. The suffering that goes on behind closed doors on an ordinary suburban street while the world spins on is something most people never think about.

In the hospital setting we were rarely cognizant of our patient's socio-economic status or the details of his or her lifestyle. Patients, dressed in identical blue-and-white checked gowns and resting in matching hospital beds, quickly blended in with all the other suffering humans on the ward. But in the home, stark variations stood out. I made visits to glorious abodes in the wealthiest neighborhoods in town, houses of patients who employed gardeners to care for the surrounding acreage. I also cared for patients whose residences were more hovel than house –plywood lean-tos lacking plumbing and basic sanitation. Death, illness, and suffering made no distinctions—young, old, pauper or prince, every age and class fell victim.

Sharon was a forty-two-year-old alcoholic. After an evening of heavy drinking, she rolled her car on a country road and broke her neck. Trapped in a deep ravine, invisible to passing cars, and unable to move to extricate herself from the vehicle, she waited for days to be found. After being rescued, she was still unable to move her arms and legs, and doctors were certain that she never would again.

During a routine visit to fill in for her regular nurse, I found my patient alone, lying flat in a double bed that had been pushed into a corner of the living room of her ramshackle three-room house. Her daughter, her main caregiver, had gone on an errand and was expected back shortly. Once again Sharon waited.

It was summer, and her room was stifling. Nervous flies flitted to and fro, and Sharon, helpless to swat them away, often found herself their target. Dust from the dirt road outside wafted in through a screenless window. The room felt like a sauna – no fan, no air conditioner.

I assessed Sharon's grim situation and turned her on her side to assess her skin. I checked her vital signs, skin, and catheter. I noticed a dirty manual wheelchair against the wall and offer to help her into it, but she preferred to stay in bed. Her demeanor flat, eyes averted, back exposed, she barely looked my way.

"I don't want to go to a nursing home," she told me. Her

voice seemed to be coming from a place far away. "I'm just fine where I am. My daughter will get me up."

I looked down at her slender body. She was a pretty woman with regular features and blonde hair. I hated to leave.

But I left my patient where I found her, lying motionless in a room furnished only with a bed and a folded wheelchair, where she lay pestered by flies, baking in the stifling heat. My brief visit left me feeling as inadequate as ever. As a home health nurse I was soon to discover that a house is not always a comfy haven. Suffering frequently comes home.

A massive, comatose man slept on his back in a hospital bed in a front bedroom of a brand new condominium. Carl's metal prison nearly filled the small space. He snored like a freight train unaware of his plight, his mouth gaping open. A pouch of liquid nutrition hung on a pole by his head. The room reeked of urine, stool, and sour milk.

The patient's wife of forty years stood in the narrow space by her husband's side, her back pressed against the wall. Ellen was a petite woman with a crown of permed silver hair. She looked at me with small eyes, standing back as far as she could from the side rails. One look and I knew she was overwhelmed. One look and I knew that she was living an impossible situation. Carl had been her life for more than four decades, and now everything had changed.

I washed and turned the unconscious man's tall frame, cleaned and filled his feeding bag, and arranged for nurses' aides to come in twice a day to help with his care. I knew it wouldn't be enough. Carl's skin was currently intact, but, because his wife couldn't turn him by herself, he remained at risk for bed sores and a host of other ills that can arise from immobility, including pneumonia. At every visit I urged his wife to consider residential care, but she stared at me in silence. Grief and fear can cause this kind of inertia. Like an animal frozen in the glare of oncoming headlights, Ellen didn't react. My words floated over her head and dissipated into the air above the vaulted ceiling of her beautiful new living room. Because I was filling in for another nurse, I never saw Ellen or Carl after that day.

But not every case was so tragic. One day orders arrived from a local urologist to visit a woman for the insertion of a urinary catheter. Her husband greeted me at the door. I was surprised to see the patient ambulatory and looking so well. She showed me to a twin bed set up in the living room. I was immediately taken aback by this arrangement, wondering why the doctor had ordered a catheter and why the patient was sleeping in the living room. Imaginary warning bells began to ring.

Before I'd finished my questions, the patient began undressing. She quickly shed her slacks and underwear and lay on her back on the mattress, legs spread, waiting for me to proceed. Her husband watched from behind a counter in their galley kitchen. I asked if he would like to leave the room. He declined. I worked quickly, with the uncomfortable feeling that I was participating in the couple's sexual fantasies. Before I left the home, I was sure of it.

Although nurses have long been the fodder for sexual jokes and innuendos, the issue of sex seldom presents itself so overtly as this. An unwanted advance, an untimely erection, a patient's occasional inappropriate sexual comments—these things happened. Medical professionals often have to touch, probe, or invade places that are personal, and we're trained to be and to feel all business when patient care requires this kind of intimacy. The ease with which even the most uncomfortable procedures are done and sensitive topics addressed arises from the immense variety of situations that turn up on the job with regularity. This familiarity with the human body and its functions often colors the exchanges between doctors and nurses, which tend to be explicit and sometimes shock those outside the medical field. Sometimes they can seem very insensitive and disrespectful of the humanity of the person and dignity of the human body. Humor in the face of another's misfortune has always bothered me.

Sexual issues also turned up with staff. During the decade I worked as a hospital nurse, the mostly-male doctors often made off-color jokes, suggestive comments, and even overt advances. I remember feeling a man's arms grab me from behind as I stood mixing IVs at a counter in the supply room and being surprised to find a dark and hairy doctor taking inappropriate liberties. I did what came naturally when faced with this type of brazen behavior and elbowed him *hard* in the chest communicating my displeasure with unmistakable clarity.

Before the advent of the term "sexual harassment," women often dealt with these incidents on their own. As young women in the 1970s, we took action to address out-of-line conduct without support from the hospital administration. This type of elbow-intervention was direct and effective and rarely needed to be repeated. If it did, a second harder stabbing usually did the trick. Lucky for me there were no repercussions.

Situations with sex that surfaced during my long nursing career seldom shocked me. This is one of the gifts of medicine: the ability to talk to and touch strangers in crisis, to accept them where they are when they arrive despite where they've been, and to try to make the best of whatever comes. I sometimes see this acceptance as one of the more *holy* aspects of the helping professions.

The uneasy situation with the catheter patient stands alone, unexpected in its audacity. I chalked the uncomfortable episode up to inexperience, noted my impressions in the case file, and reported them to the doctor. Human behavior reveals endless variations on a theme. Once again, most seasoned nurses find it hard to be shocked.

Unlike that raunchy couple, most of my patients in home health were very sick, many facing death. Hospice programs, still in their infancy, weren't widely available during this era. Even in the late 1970s, end-of-life care often fell to the family alone with brief visits from the home health nurses and aides. This proved the main takeaway from my short stint in home health. Many years later I would think about this time of my life and say a silent prayer for the legions suffering, unseen in the back rooms on the back roads all over the word, and for the families that care for them.

But it wasn't long before my full-time public health position drew to a close, and none too soon. Tom and I were preparing for the birth of our first child. Although I was excited and ready, it was hard to leave nursing behind. For the time being I accepted a job answering the phone for the Home Health Agency on weekends. This was an easy way to keep working—monitoring messages on Saturdays and Sundays, offering advice, and occasionally making a home visit to replace a catheter or consult with a patient's family. I continued taking calls on weekends through the end of my pregnancy and after the baby was born. On weekdays I saw one regular patient in her home.

Vicky's apartment was a few blocks from our house. She was a short, overweight girl in her early twenties, suffering from a congenital disease that left her body, arms, and legs encrusted with thick growths, which required daily scrubbing to remove dead skin. Her body was hard to look at—covered with bumpy lesions like a diseased oak tree, encrusted with tiny scales that flaked oily confetti on her clothing, furniture, and carpet. Dealing with this condition proved all the more challenging because Vicky was also developmentally disabled.

Vicky always answered the door in her bathrobe, and, after polite conversation, we headed for her bathtub with a surgical brush in hand. The brush's plastic bristles, coated with special soap, helped abrade the unwanted scales and cleanse her skin. This unpleasant never-ending chore required a variety of approaches to encourage her cooperation. Vicky had lifelong problems and educating her on her hygiene issues was part of my job. I despaired at the daily burdens she bore.

We fell into a regular routine. I employed a number of creative tactics to distract Vicky's attention from the distasteful task of caring for her skin: songs, games, anything that worked.

Vicky responded well to these simple methods. After her bath we slathered cream over her extremities and covered them with knitted tube bandages to keep the medications in place. When I left her home, Vicky always gave me a hug. When I finally turned her case over to another nurse, it was hard to say goodbye. I'd cared for her as I would care for a child.

I look back on this period of life as tutoring for motherhood. Little did I know how similar nursing and mothering would be.

Chapter 16

Nurse as Mother

Sunbeams stream through snowy curtains, bathing the mint green walls of the nursery in bright light. It's a hot summer Saturday, and a swamp cooler hums in the window overlooking the backyard where my husband labors. The smell of new-mown grass wafts into the room. My three-month-old daughter wakens, and I reach deep into the crib to lift her tiny form from amidst a tangle of yellow gingham. My beautiful baby beams as I plop her onto the soft cushion of the changing table to unsnap her sleeper. Her chubby legs pump as she babbles, and I babble back. I'm her mother.

* * * * * *

Baby Natalie was born easily, belying the months of tortuous worry that consumed her mother during what could be described as a neurotic pregnancy. All during the nine months of gestation I poured over all the available literature on natural childbirth and other choices in the quest for a perfect, safe delivery experience. Despite this goal, I was never sure I'd reached the ideal level of readiness.

In 1980, the days of simple trust in the decisions of doctors and medical staff were waning in American society in general as people began demanding more participation in decisions about their care. As a nurse I was savvy to all the things that could go wrong during pregnancy and childbirth. Used to looking at all health interventions with a critical eye, it was even harder for me to submit to the medical establishment. Although my obstetrics experience in nursing school was limited to two weeks, I knew too much.

When my mother gave birth in the 1950's, she had no choice but to accept general anesthesia during labor and acquiesce to two weeks of hospital bed rest after delivery, but women of my era were beginning to assume more control over what happened to them and their babies before, during, and after the birth. To medicate or not to medicate? Episiotomy or not? Breast or bottle? The options were overwhelming. Elaborate birthing rooms with elegant décor, Jacuzzis, and champagne, still lay in the future, but even during the 1980s women were starting to drive their doctors crazy with demands for special music, ambient lighting, and previously unheard of twists to the birthing experience like underwater births and camcorders in the delivery room.

I'm now thankful for the youthful hubris that duped me into thinking I was in control, that things would go as planned, and that my expectations would be met. Like countless parents before me, I had no idea what I was getting into. Does any new parent really know what they've signed up for? If not for these innocent beginnings, would we ever so heartily embrace parenthood and its lifelong commitments of love and sacrifice? Would we dare to love that much?

At our first real meeting in the hospital, the nurses wheeled Natalie into my room in a clear acrylic bassinet. Eager hospital workers routinely took possession of newborns at delivery during this era, and doled them out to their anxious mothers for brief scheduled visits. A visiting friend and I looked down at my daughter's tiny form swaddled in a pink bunting. Her newborn face peeked out from her flannel cocoon. She screamed, her face mottled, red, and scrunched with obvious distress. Overcome with motherly awe, I lifted her gently to begin our lifelong relationship.

The parallels between nursing and motherhood soon hit with full force, and I fell into step, at ease with my new role. As countless women have done through the ages, my baby's health and happiness became my first priority. I bathed her and encouraged her to feed and get her rest. I responded to her calls for help, taught her to deal with frustration, and gave her advice. She didn't want to have her diaper changed or to be strapped in a car seat, but I knew better. I encouraged her cooperation and enforced rules to ensure her health. I followed doctor's orders and gave her medicines.

Although these jobs came easily, Natalie's infancy was anything but smooth because she developed infant colic. Face beet red, legs drawn up, her tiny mouth periodically opened to emit piercing screams through most of her waking hours. Although colic is a common and benign newborn problem, the frequent prolonged bouts of fretful crying jangled everyone's nerves. Google colic today and you'll find thousands of websites offering suggestions for coping: music, medications, massage, and a myriad of panaceas to address parental frustration and waning mental health. But in 1980 we were mostly on our own. Natalie cried. Sometimes we cried together.

One night during a party our physician friends and their wives offered their help, and we passed our swaddled newborn around a circle of medical professionals for consultation. One by one they rocked, cuddled, and cooed little Natalie to no avail. Her distressing cries soon began to get on everyone nerves. One by one the doctors and their spouses gave up and handed our screaming infant back with baffled consternation and relief. No one had a plausible explanation for Natalie's distress. No one had any answers. "We don't know what causes it, but colic should run its course," said one compassionate doctor friend. "Just wait."

During my baby's infrequent moments of peace, I was the mother I want to be. In the early morning hours after a successful feeding, Natalie slept quietly, and I could hear myself think about how far we'd come. I remembered her first smile, the curve of her body against my chest in the front pack as I rocked side to side, and the sweetness of her young skin.

At this point I was blissfully unaware of the medical issues that had yet to arise, all the consultations that lay ahead, or the impact my daughter's health would have on our family, relationships, and her future. Although it's been over thirty years, that brief most ordinary scene at the changing table often comes to mind, because it was the last moment of innocence before discovery. Like so many other good and bad things that happen in life, it's a picture that punctuates. It will forever mark a potent moment in time—*a beginning and an end.*

That was the day I discovered that something was wrong with my newborn. It would take years to give it a name. The doctors' advice would often sound the same as what Tom and I heard that night at the party: "We don't know. Just wait."

* * * * * * *

"Looks like mosquito bites," the pediatrician opined at our first visit after the discovery of an angry rash on Natalie's legs and torso. Quite unsure of the plausibility of this assessment, Tom and I listened to the doctor's sincere advice but continued to worry. The "spots," as we would come to call them, first discovered on that glorious summer morning, became a regular part of our family's daily life. Every day new fiery bumps appeared and soon spread out turning into purple bruises. Daily fevers of unknown origin plagued Natalie and thus her parents. When her condition didn't clear, medical experts from a variety of disciplines were called in for consultation, and we traveled on weekdays to various teaching hospitals and medical centers in search of a diagnosis.

"Panniculitis," said one dermatologist. "Inflammation of

the fat." Packs of doctors circled, palpated, and tested Natalie to screen her for a variety of ills. Over and over blood was drawn. A biopsy offered no explanation as to cause or treatment. No one could determine what was wrong.

And so we carried on from day to day. The frequent fevers and the spreading spots continued. Pictures of her babyhood show her smiling face dotted with purplish marks, some as large as a half dollar. Our bruised infant daughter chomped on her Happy Meal unaware that an elderly woman sitting across from our booth in McDonald's, her lipsticked mouth pruned with disapproval, was glaring at her parents with silent accusations of child abuse. Not so silent accusations would surface at daycares and schools for years to come. We would be asked to leave the swimming pool because Natalie's rash "might be contagious" and concerned teachers would send Natalie to the school counselor to explain her bruises. Her daily fevers continued with wrenching regularity.

There's a common saying that the shoemaker's children have no shoes. Most medical families will agree that this adage aptly applies to physician's families in regard to their medical care. It may be a form of protective denial that leads to a skewed objectivity or a pathological reluctance to admit vulnerability, but complaints voiced at home in medical families are often informally seen as inconsequential, and the tincture of time is prescribed out of hand. For a doctor's family, treatment for *any* ailment may be long in coming. At some point after Natalie turned one year old, we stopped looking for answers. We treated her fevers and spots with aspirin and Tylenol and tried not to think.

But one morning Natalie awoke, not only with chicken pox, but with joints so swollen she that Tom had to carry her to the bathroom. The severity of these latest symptoms shocked us into action and spurred us to arrange an appointment with a yet another rheumatologist. The doctor could see us in one week. Of course, by that time the pox had cleared and the swelling disappeared. When the day came to drive north for the appointment, I started to have second thoughts.

"Let's turn around, Tom. I really don't want to know what's wrong," I said as we talked in the car on the way to the doctor.

I glanced back at our petite four-year-old daughter safely strapped in her car seat, intently perusing a story book. She looked the picture of contentment. I was full of fear.

"We have to find out. Now's the time," my sensible husband replied with authority, as he continued to drive north. For this brave decision I will be forever grateful.

As providence would have it, the doctor my husband chose for the consultation, Dr. Rennabaum, was new to northern Idaho, having recently moved from a university program back East. His extensive experience in pediatric rheumatoid disease would prove to be a real plus. Minutes after examining Natalie, he advised us that her sight was in serious jeopardy due to swelling around her optic nerves. She could go blind. He offered a tentative and plausible diagnosis: an extremely rare condition called early-onset sarcoidosis (EOS).

EOS is considered to be a genetic disease that affects patients in early childhood and will become worse if left untreated. Patients suffer from a combination of painful skin bumps, arthritis, uveitis (eye inflammation), and intermittent fevers. A gene on the fifteenth chromosome, which encodes a protein essential for the immune-inflammatory response, does not function properly, and patients experience chronic inflammation with clusters of inflammatory cells, called granulomas, which may disrupt the normal structure and functioning of various tissues and organs. Natalie's EOS was a result of a random genetic mutation.

As is so often the case with chronic illness, the diagnosis does not make life easier. The painful spots had a name—erythema nodosum—but they would keep appearing for life. Daily fevers, as high as 103.6, would continue to spike, making Natalie cranky and miserable. Stomach and joint pain would wreak havoc with her diet and activity and affect her growth. The drug she needed to take to control the symptoms of her disease (prednisone) came with numerous side effects that would alter her appearance and plague her with mood swings.

But the medicine preserved Natalie's sight. After a short course of steroids, the inflammation around her optic nerves cleared. The only evidence of the seriousness of her eye condition was minimal scarring seen only by an optometrist. Her vision remained unaffected.

Dr. Rennabaum smiled at us a few days after we began prednisone. He looked upward as if in prayer as he told us that Natalie was responding well to treatment. His broad face reflected an emotion close to ecstasy. "Natalie is exquisitely sensitive to prednisone," he said. "This bodes well." He'd told us that other children with her condition were not so lucky. Some died.

I will replay this moment and those hopeful words in the tape of my memory for the rest of my life.

One morning I was dressing four-year-old Natalie when I noticed a fine rash on her wrists and forearms. Alarmed, I examined her all over and called my husband at his office. "Tom, Natalie has petechiae on her arms and ankles," I told my husband with a composure I didn't feel.

At first Tom was incredulous, but I was insistent. "I'll call you back," Tom said hastily. As medical professionals, we knew that this type of rash was a serious symptom. But consistent with the typical dynamics of a medical family's denial complex, it took both of us time to assimilate the information. Several minutes later Tom called.

"Natalie needs to come in to get some blood drawn," he said in a strangely professional voice tinged with panic.

For once, tincture of time was not an option. We went in for the blood test, and less than an hour later Tom was on the phone—this time with urgency in his voice. "Natalie's platelets are seven thousand. She's at risk of serious bleeding with any injury. Don't let her fall or hit her head. We're taking her to Spokane."

The hospital was about an hour and a half away, but the car trip sped past in a blur. Only one memory of that frantic car ride survives. Our emotions were in overdrive. As we neared the hospital I felt my bladder about to burst. Tom pulled into a city park but the bathroom was closed and he suggested I find a bush. This was an emergency in every sense of the word. I didn't protest.

The pediatric ward of Deaconess Hospital was located on the sixth floor, and, shortly after we left the elevator, a nurse ushered us to a large room with six beds. We soon learned that this room was called "the leukemia ward." There were other children in the beds, some of them bald. I knew they were there, but I didn't really see them. Several of their hovering parents approached to welcome us. Tom and I paced around Natalie.

A team of doctors came to whisk our little girl to a procedure room next door to harvest a sample of bone marrow from her hip for testing. Tom and I knew that this was a painful procedure. The doctors told us to wait in the playroom across the hall from the site where the test would take place. We sat in tiny chairs at a tiny table amidst piles of well-worn toys for what seemed like hours. We didn't talk. I tried not to think of my child hurting. I tried not to listen for her cries. I tried not to think about leukemia.

Soon the medical staff appeared to tell us that Natalie didn't have leukemia. Her problem stemmed from a viral illness that had temporarily destroyed her platelets; the treatment would be more prednisone. A nurse came to ask us to remove our belongings from the leukemia ward. We were moving to a private room.

I felt the parents of the other patients in the large room staring as Tom and I entered to collect Natalie's clothes and blanket. No one came up to us. No one said anything as we walked past. Their heavy silence echoed down the hallway. Leukemia was not in our cards. We didn't join the club. Although I was overcome with relief, I also felt that old familiar nagging sadness. Why were we so lucky?

Except for surgery to remove her spleen my daughter's childhood held no further serious medical emergencies. Her daily life continued to include pain and fevers, and her family tried to cope. Symptoms were helped with low dose prednisone, and we made it a goal to give her as little as possible. She complained of stomach pain and wouldn't eat. We resorted to mixing instant breakfast with half-and-half and to frequent nagging. Candy was the only thing that went down easy. She grew to four feet ten inches tall and weighed less than one hundred pounds.

Contact sports were out of the question, but she competed on the swim team, became an accomplished ballerina, and had perfect attendance in school. She went on to teach in Rome, earn a master's degree in elementary education, and was accepted to medical school. Through it all, chronic disease was her constant burden but bore it and continues to bear it with grace.

In every life there will be some suffering that can't be relieved. We know this. But when a form of daily misery strikes a child, it's so hard to understand. All children seem to share the naive certainty that their parents are in control—that they will soothe the "owies," solve the problems, and make things right. When help doesn't succeed, when all we can do is keep on keepin' on, there can be the loss of something precious—a trust. Pain has been part of Natalie's daily life and her parents have been powerless to do anything about it

For years I saw my role as the tough mom, pushing the three Ps: pills, palliative comfort care, and perseverance. As a nurse I'd become well-practiced in getting reluctant patients to cooperate with needed therapies and move ahead. My propensity to deny my emotions helped me to hide my own grief and push through moment by moment, day by day. But my daughter's pain became an ever-present third party in our relationship, an unwelcome interloper that imposed its calls for attention all through her childhood. Tom and I took our roles as her parents seriously:

Tom as the comforter and me as the taskmaster. This sometimes drove a wedge between us.

Single scenes from my life as Natalie's mother pop into my mind now and again. That moment at the changing table when I was still blissfully unaware of her illness and what the future held; a time when my tears finally broke through at her bedside after elective surgery to remove her spleen, when doctors thought she might have to return to the operating room; and one glorious moment, watching her dance on stage, a picture of beauty and grace.

On the day we finally gave all her medical school study books to Goodwill, the air hung heavy with unspoken sadness. Her acceptance letter had come weeks before, but her illness played a part in her decision to decline, and her childhood dream of becoming a doctor disappeared. Thoughts of *what if* still bring back swells of sorrow.

I know many parents have these thoughts as they look into the eyes of their children with disabilities. In 1955, my husband's sister Marianne suffered a brain injury during birth when the umbilical cord wrapped around her neck leaving her intellectually impaired. She looks like Tom's other sister, and, like all her siblings, she loves music, animals, and family connections. It's hard not to see her and sometimes think: *If only things had been different.* But different will never be an option. We play with the cards we're dealt. And we love the one we're with and help them bloom.

A scene from *Autobiography of a Face* by Lucy Grealy resonates. It speaks of a fragile moment between the author and her mother as nine-year old Lucy faced chemotherapy for cancer of the jaw. In her book Lucy recalls a moment when she looked up to see tears welling in her mother's eyes and suddenly saw that her mother was suffering too. Perhaps some are shocked that Lucy didn't know that her mother hurt, not because of her, but for her. But I'm not surprised.

I'm not sure Natalie knows how much grief I keep inside,

or, like Lucy's mother, how I suffered with her. The nurse in me saw my stoicism as a way to empower my daughter to be strong. Like so many instances with my own mother, I felt my daughter's pain, but I chose action as a way to cope. In the end, Lucy's epiphany did little to help her. Knowing that her mother shared her pain did nothing to take it away. This is one thing I learned in nursing school.

I sometimes feel I will never be surprised again when the assiduously crafted curtains are too short, projects wither and fail, good intentions go bad, or when disaster falls hard out of nowhere. Most lives are peppered with times when careful plans are kicked to the curb; times when expectations so arduously anticipated fall flat and we find ourselves on bumpy paths to unexpected and unfamiliar destinations. My friend J.D, diagnosed with multiple sclerosis in his early twenties, explained this to me one day. How a new road map came with his MS diagnosis, leading him to a places he never wanted to go, and how he still struggles to adapt and accept his new destination. I know couples for whom parenthood came with just such a detour to a foreign land, who face difficult diagnoses for their children with courage and fortitude.

All my anxieties about Natalie's health continue to be seasoned by time. My expectations have mellowed. In many ways, just living has taught me to let go. Perhaps my daughter and the myriad of courageous people I've known have helped me in this regard. These are people who have faced their individualized afflictions (and those of their children) with resignation and tireless faith as their lives and plans imploded on impact with bad news from the doctor, a collision with a careening car, or sudden contact with a stray bullet. These have been my teachers. As a young nurse, I offered one eight-hour shift at a time toward their recovery, trying to help make the best of whatever befell, patch things back together and help them move on. I certainly never expected that their examples would help me to see answers to the questions that plagued me or to help me face what lie ahead.

Chapter 17

❧

Grace

"The real problem is not why some pious, humble, believing people suffer, but why some do not."

The Problem of Pain
C. S. Lewis

It's an ordinary morning in July, and I've been puttering in the kitchen of our big old house in St. Maries, Idaho. My two children, Natalie, age three, and Neal, a toddler, are roaming the house between our dining-room-turned-playroom and the kitchen as I keep busy with mundane chores. Teaching evening Lamaze classes has become my new nursing venue, but during the day I'm a stay-at-home mom.

Plastic milk jugs full of pie cherries from our backyard trees sit on the counter by the sink. I plan to start pitting them for canning but first decide to run to the laundry room to fold clothes and dump a load of cloth diapers into the dryer. I push the start button and return to the kitchen.

Suddenly I am aware of a pattering noise over my head – a sound coming from the roof. What's that? I scurry out the back door to investigate, unaware of what's transpired.

To my horror I see my fourteen-month-old son hanging from the eaves of the second story roof of our house. Dressed in a gray sweat suit, his diaper peeks out above the elastic of his tiny pants as he lies on his stomach, legs swinging over the edge of the roof. He's kicking like mad, trying to find a step to climb down. He's scaled the ladder that my husband left out to check the chimney. My baby is dangling from the second story over solid cement.

"Don't move!" I yell, as I shimmy up the ladder, scamper across the roof and grab his infant elbows and hoist him to safety. There are no words to describe what I feel at this moment. I sit on that shingled roof for some time holding my perfect child tight to my chest, rocking and repeating aloud an involuntary mantra: "Oh, my God. Oh, my God." I can't believe that Neal is okay. I can't believe that I caught him before he fell. I don't move for some time. When I do, I lift my head and look up.

The memory of that comatose baby girl lying in her crib in a Texas children's hospital forms as I sit there on the roof. I see her face ringed with blonde curls like Neal's. The babe's mother ran to answer the phone—just a moment's lapse. Too late, her parents found her face down in the family swimming pool, their baby gone. This image from my past comes vivid and unbidden and lets me know I'm a sister to all those who have lost children in accidents. It could have been me.

* * * * * * *

In 1900 my grandfather Ernest Prufer fell through the ice while skating near his home in Bonn, Germany. Eight-year-old Grandpa felt the icy cold sapping his strength as he struggled to get out of the water, when an older brother, who happened to look his way, skated over from far across the huge lake, seized his arms, and with much effort pulled him to safety. Years later, after sailing around the world many times over, Grandpa would relate the details of this event in his understated way, always expressing thanks for the gift of life. It was one of those stories that reminded us of the fragile nature of our existence and how so much can depend on a single, solitary, seemingly insignificant moment. Something as small as the breeze or a sound might have caused Grandpa's brother to skate the other way and thus changed the future for all of us. I remember my fascination with this tale as a child. I realized that if my eight-year-old Grandpa had died, I would have never been born.

My life resonates with similar stories of critical moments when fate hinged on perfect timing, and/or seemingly insignificant details that changed the story. Grandma Mitzel boarded a boat in steerage headed for New York City on April 12, 1912, the same day another ship, the *Titanic*, began her ill-fated voyage. A teenage daughter, on her own maiden voyage in the family car, overcorrected and rolled four times cracking her neck at C-2 but sparing her spinal cord. And this author once mysteriously maneuvered her vehicle around four semis that hemmed her in, to slip onto a sandy truck ramp when the brakes failed traveling down the steep Lewiston grade. In all these instances, things dropped into place like well-placed notes in a musical masterpiece or mosaic tiles in an ancient fresco, miraculously leading to beautiful endings.

But sometimes the skater drowns, the ship sinks to the bottom of the sea, the sunroof doesn't collapse into a V- shape and the teen is paralyzed, the truck ramp is too far away, the luck isn't good, and the break never comes. Sometimes the child has leukemia.

Our existence in the world often seems to be a strange combination of happenstance and accident snapped together like a bizarre puzzle, the picture of which remains obscure. Is it God's mysterious tapestry that will someday be revealed from the other side, or is it random unbridled luck? Either way, despite the eager scramble for control of our mortal lives, suffering seems inevitable. Not all choices are ours to make.

Whether good or bad, stuff happens. And we can't make sense of it. We can't figure it out.

The revelation I experienced on the roof that morning with Neal would not go away. At the heart of my torment was a chronic and reverberating angst over the unfairness of life. If there was a God, how could he let suffering happen in such a random way? Why had I been spared?

I'd made my share of mistakes on the road oft traveled. Sins of volition and omission—I'd chalked up a sizeable list that I always preferred not to enumerate. In that instant on the roof, I was startled to find myself looking at the issue from the flip side of Rabbi Harold S. Kushner's classic book *Why Do Bad Things Happen to Good People.* Says C. S. Lewis, "The real problem is not why some pious, humble, believing people suffer, but why some do not." The guilt that had surfaced so many times as I cared for my patients once again washed over me, this time without mercy.

Many years after that moment on the roof in Idaho, as Tom and I drove Neal to Idaho to begin his freshman year of college, we passed through St. Maries. An older gentleman stopped us to share a story of a traumatic scene he'd witnessed in 1983. Driving down College Avenue on his way to work, he saw a small baby in a gray jersey sweat suit hanging from the eaves of a two-story house. Shaking, he pulled his car over and watched as the child's frantic mother climbed the ladder to make the rescue. Like the mother, the man sat for some time collecting his thoughts. And, like the mother, he also looked up.

It would be some time before I realized this was where I would find my answers. It would be years before the religion of my childhood would show itself in a new light. But there would be no blazing light-bulb moment. No lightning epiphany. I would have to live as Rainer Maria Rilke advised in his *Letters to a Young Poet*: "Live my questions," and "Live the way to the answers." I would have to relive the scenes of patients and experiences from my past, meld them with experiences yet to

114

come, and eventually find my way back to the place where I started. In the words of T. S. Eliot, I would arrive there "and know the place for that first time."

* * * * * * *

An ambulance was screaming toward us and my husband pulled over as the speeding vehicle streaked past. For a few seconds we both felt derailed. Maybe it's because of our medical background, but the sound of a roaring siren never fails to make us pause. The blare always jars us from our comfortable thoughts, intruding with an unwelcome reminder of our own fragile hold on life. Perhaps it's because we've lived in small towns for so many years. Unless it was noon, the wail of the horn from its high post by the post office of our small community often meant that one of our own had gone down.

The siren blew one day as I was standing by the football field with a group of high school students waiting for the school bus. Everyone stopped. A blanket of stillness descended over the normally rowdy group as we looked at each other. In the eyes of those teenage kids I saw a knowing sadness that mirrored my own. *Who was it? What's happened?* On that particular day two people lost their lives: a sixteen-year-old boy named Paul and his grandfather, victims of one of the very real hazards of living in rural America—roads with soft gravel shoulders. Sirens make people in a small towns stop. That's just the way it is.

On another afternoon when another one of our young people died, we also heard the wailing alarm and waited to hear. The awful news was quick in coming. A first grader, riding his bike in front of his house on the highway, had been struck by a woman driving her car into town. The boy's broken body had been rushed to the emergency room, and the staff—all of whom knew him and his family—worked to save him to no avail.

Of course, the townspeople rallied around the grieving family, but, as with all deaths, there came a time when the memorials and tributes ended; condolence cards ceased to arrive, and words of comfort became uneasy silence. The hugs, help, and hot dishes stopped coming. People no longer talked about what happened. Occasionally someone mentioned something about the child's love of bugs or his happy smile. But life went on; only the silent grief remained.

One of the survivors of this tragedy who continued to grieve was the woman who hit the boy. Also a member of our small town family, her name was published in the local paper. I remember learning the horrible news. She was someone I'd known for some time – a woman who suffered, mainly from poverty in the physical, relational, and spiritual sense. A generational legacy of pain and neglect had scarred her childhood and was beginning to play itself out in the lives of her many children. Divorced and struggling to survive, she scrambled to house, feed, and clothe herself and her large family. Living on the edge of disaster and oppressed by the tyranny of the moment, simple things like dental care, which so many of us take for granted, went by the wayside. It hurt to know that now she had yet one more trouble to add to her already burdensome load. I knew that accidents happen. They'd happened to me.

One day in the grocery, many years after that day on the roof with my son, I saw this woman. She came up to me as I stood by the dairy case at the local grocery store. We knew each other. Our lives had crossed many times through my work in public health, at the school, and on the intersecting paths that comprise small town life. Her acne-scarred face lit up and her smile glowed despite her blackened and missing teeth. She looked into my eyes with such a frank hunger for acceptance and love that I was moved to touch her. She grabbed my body and hugged me. She hugged me for all she was worth.

The woman's grief poured into me, just like that time so many years ago when that anguished husband barreled toward me in the hallway of the private hospital with his overwhelming need. But this time something was different.

In this woman's utter brokenness, I saw myself. By some kind of miracle, instead of unadulterated pain tinged with fear, a sense of her longing and emptiness flowed into me, and I knew it was also mine. Like so many pivotal moments, this one sang as if from a celestial choir. This sister's pain was also my own. It revealed a longing we shared. We were empty in a place only love could fill. As I stood there in the supermarket in her arms, I began a new path. I began to heal. I began to see the way.

Chapter 18
❧

Memories

M emories have taken a bad rap of late, and much of the criticism seems justified. Neuroscientists have declared that almost all memories are simply memories of memories—recollections seen through the filter of today. With each remembrance, the mind adds unique perceptions and acquired knowledge, changing mental images and stories in subtle ways that distort their purity. As I write this memoir, I have to consider these concepts despite the discomfort they cause. The scenes I recall may have lost a modicum of accuracy, and their interpretation may have been colored by time and experience. But movies don't lie. Perhaps that's why I find them so disconcerting.

When I was five, my parents bought an 8mm movie camera that they used to make films of family get-togethers. With both sets of grandparents and my dad's huge extended family of first, second, and third cousins living within minutes of our hometown on the edge of Queens, we spent almost every weekend with relatives. Any excuse to celebrate would do. A birthday, special anniversary, or holiday and off we'd head to Alley Pond Park for a softball game and picnic lunch or a drive to Bayside to spend an afternoon gorging on one of Grandma Mitzel's hearty feasts. Every family gathering offered yet another chance to document the mundane weekend activities of our ordinary lives on black-and-white film.

We watched these silent flicks on a collapsible screen in the tiny living room of my grandparent's second-floor apartment in Maspeth, making bunnies with our hands in the light of the projector between reels and enjoying our own version of stardom, supremely entertained. What could be better?

Several years ago my sister transferred these choppy cinematic creations from film to DVD. Initially I embraced the opportunity to reminisce, but minutes into watching I found myself reaching for the off button. So many things had changed in the five decades since those movies were made, and somehow it was hard to take.

The stick-thin eight-year-old me in ponytail and pedal pushers doing cartwheels in the grass is now a jowly matron with gray hair and a failing body. The annoying curly-haired baby sister toddling toward the camera, long ago morphed into an adult who still consistently pushes all my buttons. Jolly Grandma Mitzel with her impish eyes and histrionic personality, and my stoic bear-like German Grandpa with his gruff exterior and tender heart both passed away over forty years ago. Their images, now frozen on a plastic disc, evoke memories that will remain only as long as those who knew them can remember.

These home movies offer evidence of both the good and the bad of my childhood. Some images I'd rather forget: Dad, staggering and bleary-eyed after one too many Mai Tais; rotund Uncle Ernie's screaming fits laden with profanity directed toward his pitiful mutt named Bum; and Uncle Dick's vitriolic rants admonishing us kids to "get lost."

The DVDs of these times caught on film over five decades ago now gather dust as a crude documentary of a childhood on Long Island in the 1950s, but their greater value is in their revelation of the fleeting nature of life. The main characters, most now gone from the earth, provide this testimony. There are no reruns for our time on this planet. Life is fragile.

Awareness of our existence is what makes us human. Minds housed in fragile bodies—this is the human dilemma. Nowhere is the fleeting nature of our existence on this planet more painfully evident than in the practice of medicine.

For many years my husband and I attended medical dinners funded by drug companies promoting new medicines. Although currently out of favor as a result of protests by consumer advocates, these "free" dinners usually included valuable talks by local specialists on a variety of topics and were considered perks of the job. One memorable evening, the drug salesmen brought in a cardiologist with up-to-date information about the latest clot-busting treatments for heart attack. Our little group of medical professionals and their wives listened intently at the same time chowing down on hefty steaks and baked potatoes smothered with butter, sour cream, and all the fixings. Every person, including the heart specialist, ordered the same high-fat feast. Doctors and nurses know better than most that life is short, and medicine has a huge number of limits. We often don't follow our own advice.

In fact, although medical science has made great strides in the treatment and prevention of disease and can often *prolong* life, it often fails to have any answers at all for an infinite number of maladies that affect the human body. This is a truth well-known by the afflicted.

Marlena lives in an alternate reality without language. For unknown reasons she was born with severe autism, and medicine offers little in the way of help. Grace found out she has systemic lupus. Although drugs blunt the effects of her immune system run amok, the damage to her organs will continue. Peggy fell off her horse and languishes in a nursing home in a permanent vegetative state. She'll receive all her meals through a tube in her stomach and never regain full consciousness. My daughter Natalie's altered gene is something that currently can't be fixed. These are the cards that were dealt.

Despite crippling limitations, public expectations for the

power of modern medicine run high and seem to correlate with a tendency to gloss over the issue of human mortality. An article in the *New England Journal of Medicine* tells the story of an octogenarian's visit to the doctor. Puzzled by her experience of decreasing strength and stamina, she sought treatment at a university clinic and expressed outrage when she was informed: "Old age happens, and there's no cure." The truth is, time takes a toll on everyone's body. You can exercise, watch your diet, and take advantage of all the medical world has to offer, but you will still die. Despite this fact, people generally have high expectations and regularly undergo heart surgery, chemotherapy, and a whole host of other treatments even into their nineties and beyond with unwavering faith that doctors can keep them going. Says Cicero: "No one is so old as to think he cannot live one more year."

To have a mind that is self-aware and to know that it's housed in a body that will not last forever is the human conundrum that forces a question that science cannot answer: What is the meaning in it all? An excerpt from a poem called "Easter Sunday, 1955" by Elizabeth Spires speaks to the timeless nature of this question.

> *. . . No one has died yet.*
> *No vows have been broken. No words spoken*
> *that can never be taken back, never forgotten.*
> *I have a basket of eggs my mother and I dyed yesterday.*
> *I ask my grandmother to choose one, just one,*
> *and she takes me up—O hold me close!—*
> *Her cancer not yet diagnosed. I bury my face*
> *in soft flesh, the soft folds of her Easter dress,*
> *breathing her in, wanting to stay forever where I am.*

When I read this poem I'm transported back in time to my own Grandma Mitzel's kitchen in Queens.

There's a sauerbraten roast simmering on the stove, and

the pungent smells of red cabbage and spaetzle permeate the air. My little Austrian grandma is up to her elbows in cookie dough as she churns the buttery mixture with her hands in a shallow plastic bowl. Her stocky frame hangs over the sides of the child-sized wooden chair that she sits in at the kitchen table in her kitchen in Queens. Her puffy feet are crammed into chunky shoes, and the vest-like apron she always wears is soiled and worn. Her false teeth click as she moves her mouth with satisfaction. She is in her element.

The kitchen sink overflows with dirty dishes and the rest of the house is as unkempt as Mitzel's sparse hair, which falls in long strings onto her forehead as she cooks. Her head is down, and she occasionally lifts it to look at me and offer a taste of her work. Her sky blue eyes are twinkling, and she's barely able to contain her joy when I bite into one of her buttery confections. The cookies are silken perfection—glorious—and I know that she lives to create them. They never disappoint.

Even though I'm only five, Grandma's passion inspires me to do my own cooking. She's in the bedroom when I decide to play in her spice cabinet. I climb on the kitchen table and dump all her expensive spices into the cooking pot and add water. I mix the resultant glob of brown goo with a wooden spoon flooding the air with the scent of cinnamon and cloves. The pungent smell draws Mitzel into the room.

At first Grandma feigns shock, waving her arms and shouting in hysterical German, her flowered apron flapping, but soon her impish laughter comes in waves, and her sky-blue eyes glitter with mischief and delight. She opens her arms, and I nestle my five-year-old face in the folds of her apron. She smells of the celery and red onion that she'd been chopping for German potato salad. Her body is soft and fleshy. She accepts me. The world melts away.

* * * * * * *

"But we can't stay forever where we are. We don't even know where we are, until after we have been there, until we look back to see what happened, ten, twenty, thirty Easters later," says Forrest Church in his book *Life Lines*. I didn't know it then, but that twinkling moment as a five-year-old in my grandmother's kitchen would prove to be a blessing—a precious memory of priceless value that speaks with utter sincerity. Distorted by the present or not, it sings with truth. It screams: "This is what's important."

Elizabeth Spires' poem ends:

. . .Now my daughter steps
into the light, her basket of eggs bright, so bright.
One, choose one, I hear her say, her face upturned
to mine, innocent of outcome.

And the cycle repeats itself. I'm now almost as old as the grandma of my memories and have grandchildren of my own. A tiny picture of Mitzel dressed in blue sneakers and a flowered dress sits on the desk in my kitchen. She sports a bow on her head, and her cheeks glisten round and ruddy. Her jolly spirit comes across as if she's speaking through time, her eyes sparkling with a hidden secret.

This is one reel of memories I don't mind replaying—a remembrance of acceptance and mixed spice, butter cookies and loose emotions, letting go and loving. My grandmother's unbridled love communicated through time.

An old Bible teaching springs to life. "Only love remains, only the love we give away." As a nurse, a mother, a human being, I must remember this. And when I finally take this truth to my center, it's the beginning of a new life.

Chapter 19
❧

Regrets

*"Maybe all one can do is hope to
end up with the right regrets."*

Arthur Miller

On an ordinary morning on the job at County General in the early
1970s, I pass a colleague on my way to the med room behind
the nursing desk. We exchange polite hellos and brief conversation.
This is just a chance meeting, a fleeting instance where our frenzied
paths happen to collide as we both head to the refrigerator to get
vials of insulin. I haven't seen or talked to Cheri for weeks. As
with most of the staff at County General, we barely know each
other outside the report room. Like Clydesdales harnessed to pull
in tandem, we work separate hallways and our trajectories seldom
cross. Our status as RN team leaders means that we're always
assigned to our own team and many of us work rotating shifts.
The unrelenting nature of our workload leaves no time for sharing
stories or personal concerns. Tom works as medical student on
our floor, but no one's aware that I have a boyfriend much less of
the vacillating status of our relationship and the problems we face.
Cheri and I know each other's names and little else.

On the day in question I happen to notice her appearance. She's a beautiful woman in her early thirties with blonde hair and the zaftig body of an endomorph, but today she looked pale and much thinner, her face taut and haggard, her short uniform draped on a shrunken frame.

"Cheri, you've lost a lot of weight," I mention casually, stopping for a moment to face her. "I haven't seen you in a while."

Her eyes roll. "Yeah, I've lost weight. Pretty soon you won't be able to see me at all." She's facing me as she speaks, but her eyes drop to the floor and she backs away. Even her voice seems changed, wispy and unassuming, telegraphing a coded message that remains undeciphered as it flies past. She clutches the vial of medicine from the refrigerator and hurries down the hall. I too continue on my way.

The news of Cheri's death is announced the next morning as our teams gathered by the big med cart behind the nurse's desk. After her shift that day Cheri attached a hose to the tailpipe of her car in the garage and waited to die.

Stunned, my colleagues and I stare beyond each other's gazes, trying to make sense of what's happened.

"I think she was married and her husband was having an affair," one nurse offered.

Few knew that Cheri was married let alone the anguish she bore. Had the horrendous responsibilities we faced on the job consumed our compassion for each other? Intent on dealing with the ever-pressing roster of tasks, did we fail to detect suffering that festered within our ranks?

Cheri's brief comment as we stood by the refrigerator in the med room screamed in my head and remorse rolled over me. This is one legacy of suicide.

* * * * * * *

Through all the years I worked as a nurse, I had to make decisions that would impact the well-being of the people I cared for. Many times I second guessed those choices. *Should I have called for help sooner? Did I miss a critical sign? Was there something I could or should have done? Could I have tried harder?* On the front lines of patient care, the nurse has an enormous responsibility to pick up on and report problems and significant changes to the doctor. No matter how conscientious and vigilant, there will always be times when something is missed.

As I look back on my career, I'm sometimes overcome with an aching remorse that has no solace—often for things left undone. Nothing reveals this regret like suicide.

I've known countless patients who have given their all in the effort to live. Faced with horrendous treatments and immense suffering, they pressed on hoping for life and the promise of future goodness in more time on earth. Many went down still trying. The ones who made the conscious decision to leave this world on their own terms through suicide have always been the hardest to understand. The cause is so often elusive. Was it a chemical imbalance in the nether regions of the brain resulting in the blackest of depressions, childhood trauma finally bearing its terrible fruit, or an impulsive act of volition in response to a moment of despair that demanded an escape? Perhaps an element of spiritual longing, a drive for communion with a higher being, and a yearning for a better place leads a person to take his or her own life. These are the questions that only the despairing soul can answer.

In today's world, which lauds privacy and rugged individualism, so many of us seem to bowl alone, living parallel lives with wounded places unexposed, never touching. Although it may be widely acknowledged that everyone has troubles, even intimate friends and family may have difficulty sharing their deepest heartaches and secret pain. The world applauds strength, power, and a very narrow definition of success. Not wanting to appear weak, many people choose to try to cope on their own.

Sometimes the warning of despair comes in code that can

only be deciphered in hindsight. Other times the pain is evident, but interventions fail to meet deep needs. The *if-onlys* that seem to pop up with every tragedy loom larger and heavier with suicide adding to the weight of the guilt of those left behind.

The mental image of a kindergarten teacher using rope to hang herself from the rafters of her garage was burned into my brain from stories I heard in second grade. A close relative, despairing over chronic illness, tried pills. A friend's fourteen-year-old son left the breakfast table to end his hidden suffering with his father's shotgun in the family garage. Suicide and I have history. It's touched my life on more than one occasion, and it stings like no other death. It often leaves survivors with a residue of remorse that weighs down the spirit. No matter what the circumstances, it's the hardest kind of passing.

There may be no sense of personal culpability when you didn't know the person before they made their choice. But no matter what the situation, some form of regret always seems to take center stage when suicide is involved. As a nurse, I cared for patients who made it to our post-op floor after surgeries to repair the damage of botched attempts that resulted in horrendous disabilities—an esophagus burned shut after drinking Drano, a face shot off by a gunshot to the mouth, or total paralysis from a stray bullet intended for the heart. These are the sad cases of lifelong consequences that result from trying a permanent solution to a temporary problem.

* * * * * * *

Several decades after my experience with Cheri I was standing at the window of our home in Lakeview, Oregon, watching our neighbor Kenny playing in what was left of our bountiful summer garden. He was gleaning shriveled carrots and forgotten cherry tomatoes from withering stalks and fastening them together with toothpicks to make little figures. It was something for him to do after a long day at the funeral home.

Forty-eight hours earlier on a beautiful day in October, his thirty-two-year-old mother made the decision to end her life.

On the day Kenny's mother died, I'd pulled up to the front of our house with a van full of groceries after a quick trip to Safeway. Kenny and his mom were selling lemonade at a card table on the sidewalk in front of their house across the street. The family was new to our neighborhood, and we'd never met. Although I felt the urge to go over and introduce myself, I decided to take the groceries into the house first. When I came back, the little stand was gone. Later that afternoon my husband and I saw an ambulance in front of their home. Kenny's mother was dead.

Seven-year-old Kenny came to our door and introduced himself on the afternoon after his mother's funeral. Recognizing his need for TLC and the possibility that I might provide some, he took a chance and rang our bell. He impressed me with his intelligence and amazing resiliency. This was the beginning of our relationship.

Kenny and I took long walks, sprinkling bird seed from paper cups for the coveys of quail that frequented the alleys behind our house. We walked in the cool high dessert afternoons, swinging our arms outward and up with abandon to disperse handfuls of seed while singing "Feed the Birds" from *Mary Poppins*. It felt powerful to fling the seed and watch the birds dart in for their bounty. Once our cups were empty, we would return to the garage to fill them again and again as we reveled in the freedom of this very simple activity.

Kenny loved to make forts and stores out of the couch cushions and end tables and to peruse the big box of Halloween costumes in our attic to find costumes for our dog. He had an uncanny knack of crafting primitive machines he'd seen in children's science books at the library. No one was more resourceful in hunting down the required rubber bands, corks, and various doodads needed to complete a working peanut dispenser or a cardboard periscope. With a tendency toward perfectionism, he completed every project he started with a stick-to-it manner that I envied.

Most afternoons, Kenny helped me cook dinner. In quiet moments we made a ceremony of lighting a candle, which we called "the candle of forgiveness," to remember his mother and acknowledge the feelings that plague those who are grieving. We had some serious talks about what happened. When it seemed right, we visited his Mom's grave, hunting for her headstone under a layer of crusty snow and sharing memories. At times like these, our words were few.

Kenny found comfort in our black Labrador and spent hours just lying with her on her bean bag bed in the family room. Pneuma, a docile dog, proved supremely accommodating. Kenny molded himself to her body as if to absorb her unconditional love. A picture of the two of them sits on my desk. In it Kenny is blissful and relaxed, reclining on the plaid dog bed with Pneuma's paws draped over his shoulders in a loving embrace— a heartbroken boy receiving acceptance and healing from a canine therapist.

The winter after Kenny's mother died, my son and a pack of his college friends came home and fled to our backyard to play in the snow. It had been a long, hard winter in the highest town in Oregon, and the berms reached the tops of the wooden slats of our backyard fence. On the day the college chums arrived, everyone was eager to have some fun after the long car ride from Idaho. Kenny had already been outside for hours, constructing tunnels in the icy crust—a castle of sorts. The college set peeled out to play.

Laughter emanated from the yard as the teens piled into the tunnels. With everyone packed inside, Kenny saw his chance. Starting from one end, he stomped across the top of his snowy creation, crushing the roof, and pelting those more than twice his age with chunks of snow.

Years later, Kenny moved away to live with relatives. I still think of his mother, loving her son enough to set up a lemonade stand and sit with him in the sun, all the while contemplating her death. I wonder if things would have been different if I'd left my groceries in the car and walked across the street, spoken to her, and reached out—the "what if" that haunts us after every suicide.

Neal and his college pals went on to graduate, marry their college sweethearts, and move into their own real castles. I often pray that Kenny will realize the same bright future despite his early experience of tragedy. But I know that his life, already caved-in in such a tender spot, will forever have a broken place.

Every death leaves its mark, but suicide is a harbor for regret. I can't help but think: *If only I'd stopped to buy some lemonade.*

* * * * * * *

We were old friends at the breakfast table enjoying a bright July morning, nursing mugs of coffee and nibbling coffee cake. The day had just begun to stretch to life, and we were easing into it, comfortable in our familiarity. Conversation came easily, and we laughed with the intimacy of our rich history together. The house was open and teeming with the cool freshness of a summer morning. A breeze blew through open doors. The air smelled of cinnamon and sunshine. It felt good to be alive.

But this fragile, golden moment was soon broken. I happened to look up to see an officer's bulky frame filling the doorway at the front of the house, his young figure backlit and imposing in dark blue. One hand rested on his gun belt. Although his stance was wide and assured, something told me he was afraid.

With quiet efficiency the policeman informed us that my co-worker, Sharon, was dead. She hung herself in the shed behind her house. Help came too late. He delivered these sad words with the skilled tenderness of a professional.

"It was no one's fault," he said to comfort us.

As he talked I felt my throat close. I wasn't so sure.

When I finally spoke, my words sounded hollow. I felt like I was performing a play about a woman who has just learned of her friend's death. It was a rotten play, poorly written, and I had no talent and had never rehearsed. I awkwardly watched myself on this stage. My lines, stilted and plastic, generated no effect on me or my audience. I delivered them because I had to. They were caught on tape.

No messages in code or unfortunate timing to blame this time. Sharon's mental anguish had been evident to all her knew her. Hospitalization, counseling, a cornucopia of antidepressants both new and old—all proved ineffectual in treating her slide into the darkness of major depression. Over time this dark abyss sucked her down and every hand held out to help remained further and further out of reach.

We first met in October when she came into the office accompanied by our supervisor and immediately I noted something wrong. Sharon's eyes flitted from side to side when she talked as if she was trying to see who was watching. She picked at her clothing—a hint of the unrelenting anxiety attacks that plagued her. Her wiry gray hair gave her a wild look. Her baggy clothing, as loose as her fragile hold on sanity, failed to disguise her painfully thin form. She seemed perpetually uneasy.

At orientation Sharon scribbled notes on scraps of paper trying to get things down verbatim. Later, I would understand this to be the result of her inability to concentrate and her constant fear that she would miss something and make a mistake. Losing her job was not an option. A thin thread of financial solvency hung in the balance.

The two of us worked together in a small office, and it wasn't long before Sharon poured out her story: the suicide of her mother and, later, her husband, and her long ordeal with mental illness. Her pain was palpable—her frankness disconcerting. She spilled the particulars of her sex life and past relationships in wrenching detail that I would have rather not known. But sharing had no therapeutic value. Nothing I said seems to reach her. My help, like that of other friends, failed miserably. I found myself drawing back from a dark vortex that was threatening to draw me in. As the weeks and months went by, Sharon's illness became the large zoo animal in the room. Friends and family continued to reach out, but the slow slide down continued unabated. The edges of her pit were crumbling and she seemed to have nothing to hold onto.

The night after learning of her death, I dreamed of Sharon, her wispy frame hunched and miserable in a stone cave carved into the side of a building in an unnamed city. I called her name, but she wouldn't answer. The stone walls of the enclosure threatened to collapse. There was no light. She crouched in this darkness, tethered by the invisible tentacles of something that would not let her free.

My arms went limp and my feet ached with heaviness as I turned toward the light outside the cave. Once again, I was leaving as powerless as ever. There was nothing left to do but go on. In the dream I climbed in the driver's seat of a bus and began driving downhill over miles of concrete stairs directly into a public library. It was bumpy ride, but I was on a mission. As I barreled into the library, I saw a cartoonish-looking bomb on one of the oak tables. Its fuse was smoking, and I could hear it ticking. I turned to leave, but my conscience called. I couldn't ignore a bomb. I grabbed it, sped to an open field, placed it on my shoulder, and heaved with all my strength. But the heavy bomb went nowhere. It landed by my feet with a thud. I should have tried harder. There were no do-overs.

"It's no one's fault," I heard the policeman say as my mental tape played. "No one could have helped." My response echoes in the private theater of my mind: "I'm not so sure."

But time and faith will help with the issues raised here. Forgiveness is part and parcel of the message of the cross that was beginning to be real to me. Even though I think I've come to terms with it, that awful pain still smarts: in the patients I never took the time to talk to; in the places where I chose to hide in the narcosis of activity not wanting to feel; and for the times I failed to act or love enough.

If Jesus could forgive His tormentors, maybe He would forgive me.

Knowing His forgiveness maybe I could forgive myself.

Chapter 20

❧

Sick

"Now we know that if the earthly tent we live in is destroyed, we have a building from GOD, an eternal house in heaven not built by human hands.

2 Corinthians 5:1 NIV

Women become used to changing bodies. Transformation defines puberty—the overnight eruption of breasts that swell, a body that's bloated, and a uterus that cramps with monthly cycles. Then there's the enormous change that comes with pregnancy: stretch marks, weight gain, backaches, urinary urgency, and the familiar sense of loss of power over what's happening. Feminine bodies morph throughout life, undergoing various experiences of shrinking, stretching, expanding. Why should the effects of getting older be any surprise?

As I enter my sixties, my seventh decade around the sun, the mirror holds a shock. Wispy, fading hair with the texture of cotton candy that stays sculpted when wet, becomes crisp, frizzled straw, coiling like a schizophrenic broom when it's dry. Even the space between my eyebrows fuzzes with a pale, furry growth.

The bathroom cabinet bulges with age-defying powders and creams that cover, camouflage, exfoliate, and medicate. I keep that cabinet door open to avoid the mirror that reveals the wrecked visage of my former self. My skin is mottled and crackled and has the look of dried clay buffeted by years of erosion from tiny streamlets. It's dotted with pinkish eruptions that defy explanation: keratoses and suspicious ditzels that seem to detonate overnight, resulting in regular appointments with a dermatologist. Ghoulish circles puff around my eyes. Gravity pulls. Jowls jiggle when I laugh and hang tough when I don't giving me the haggard, dour appearance of a not-too-friendly older woman. Even the corners of my mouth seem to be sagging, too lazy to turn up without concentrated effort. Bunions, cracked teeth, and bleeding gums – when will it end?

The damage has also headed south. A paunch balloons, pressing against the elastic waistband I once swore I'd never wear. This hillock makes its presence known each time I feel the waistband of my pantyhose snap and roll, cascading over its bulbous expanse like a cloth avalanche. Unaccustomed to my size, I find myself trying to squeeze between the counter and the kitchen table—a space I used to navigate with ease—or into clothes that used to be loose, only to be stopped by this foreign blubbery growth, euphemistically termed a "menopot."

My flaccid upper arms, their dimpled softness compressed by stretchy fabric, are smaller clones of the ones my grandmother used when she hugged me and smothered my childish face in puffy billows that hung from the armholes of her cotton house dress. Tangles of purple dimple the doughy limbs that are now my legs, calves, and ankles, merging into what my son lovingly calls "cankles." Spidery veins snake up my thighs forming clusters of pinkish webs.

Things are out of sync. My entire sponging bulk seems to be melting, its plump shape morphing into a characteristic matron silhouette with ample bottom and pillowed bosom. All that's missing is some type of assistive device like a cane or sturdy shoes and a flowered babushka like Grandma's. These I know are coming.

* * * * * * *

Like so many women, I've spent a good part of my life hating my body. An obsession with fat and weight, which probably began at puberty, flourished after I left for college and created a kinky relationship with food that persisted through most of my twenties.

Although underweight as a child and far from overweight as an adult, my college friends and I experimented with all kinds of fad diets in pursuit of a lean and lithe look. In nursing school we downed can after can of Metracal and Sego in place of meals. We froze these Slim-Fast type libations and whipped them full of air with a hand mixer until the eight-ounce chocolate drink turned to several quarts of airy foam. The idea was to trick our brains and stomachs into thinking we were full even though the mixing-bowl size portions of chocolate mousse we were eating were just watery fluff.

The cabbage diet was another short-lived experiment. Famished after a day of classes, we rushed back to the nursing dorm to consume an entire head of cabbage—quartered, slivered, and drenched in low-calorie dressing. Shredded carrots were added on day five of the diet. Both the cabbage and the chocolate foam regimes were the frequent cause of intestinal disturbance.

Dieting in college became a community affair, and getting our provisions for the menu of the week proved immensely satisfying. Of course, we always started on Monday with a mandatory trip to the grocery to stock up on radishes, grapefruit, peach nectar, or whatever supplies were required for the *régime du jour*. It was comforting to know that the fridge was stocked with two dozen hardboiled eggs, or that a spaghetti pot full of vegetable broth was brewing on the stove, assuring us that all eating decisions, at least for the next week, were firmly determined. Such a feeling of being in control!

We cooked and ate together, savoring our common pursuit of svelteness. Between meals, the students in our group snacked on chewy, one-inch square candies called Ayds that were supposed to swell in our stomachs. We tried pretzel sticks (reportedly one calorie per stick) with sixteen ounces of water to the same end. Few of us lost weight.

But our troop of dedicated dieters remained undeterred. We burned calories just trying to chip away at the eight-ounce bricks of frozen Sego to get them chunked and ready for the mixer. Shredding piles of raw vegetables with a hand grater was a great workout. No one suffered from the more serious eating disorders of bulimia or anorexia. When we really got hungry, we ate. But, for a good part of the time, dieting consumed our thoughts.

It has been close to thirty-five years since I've been on a fad diet. The things I did when I was young seem so foolish now. When people feel like something is out of control, whether it be their weight, emotions, finances, or health, the tendency is to try to get things back in some kind of order, and the way we choose to do that has a lot to do with our personality and the social pressures bearing down on us. I attribute a lot of the silly eating routines that I followed in college and beyond to an unconscious desire to get a handle on emotions that seemed to be slipping out of control. If I couldn't change my marital status, my job situation, or the pain and panic backing up in the recesses of my troubled psyche, at least I could manage what I put in my mouth.

Although these wacky eating habits followed me through my twenties, my almost ten-year flirt with what I would term a diet disorder ended with marriage and motherhood; my issues with control stabilized. But life is never stable. Things are always changing. Learning to cope with change may prove to be one of the great accomplishments of any life.

No one can predict the future with total accuracy. Oldsters hope to avoid the common fate of Alzheimer's or the slow demise of sickly old age that seems so endemic. But no matter who we are, our health won't last indefinitely. There will come a time when our bodies, our earthly abodes, will fail.

I sometimes think that the obsession with healthcare that seems to affect so many has become just another way to gain a handle on waning control. We all are constantly bombarded by medical news stories that foster the belief that everyone can manage their health and avoid chronic disease with judicious attention to diet, exercise, and modern pharmacology and thus avoid the dreaded nursing home experience. As a member of the medical profession, I've long known that our sense of immense power and influence over our health is just an illusion.

Aching feet were the constant complaint of both my mother and grandmother. As a young girl I attributed their problems to excess weight. Grandma's four-foot nine-inch frame and fanatical love of food made her roly-poly form inevitable. Although my mother bragged that she weighed one hundred and seven pounds when she was engaged in 1946, she was also very short and had a rotund, apple-shaped body. She struggled to stay below a size 20 for most of her adult life.

I remember Grandma's labored gait as she leaned on my Grandfather's arm, plodding her way from house to car, which was her sole form of exercise. Swollen feet in thick, flesh-colored cotton socks plumped over the top of the chunky black leather shoes, which were standard footwear for women her age. Her blue-veined legs, coated with witch hazel, peeked out from under her dress and moved along with great effort.

Both my mother and grandmother regularly complained of pain in their extremities. Mom's mottled lower limbs bulged with the varicose veins she'd had since pregnancy—a constant source of embarrassment and a never-ending cause of discomfort. Part of her morning grooming routine included sponging herself with leg makeup from a large jar she kept in the medicine cabinet. As she aged, she complained more and more of aching feet and seldom walked anywhere. Her dumpling-shaped torso on swollen limbs began to look more and more like Grandma's.

Problem feet prevented both my mother and my grandmother from even such a simple physical activity as walking through the mall. In my early forties when my own feet began to hurt, I briefly worried that the problem might be genetic. *Was I literally following in their footsteps?*

At first I dismissed the genetic component. Except for pregnancy, my weight had remained in a normal range. Varicose veins had never been a problem. My girlfriends and I walked several miles every day and were known to enjoy many early morning games of tennis. I blamed my burning tootsies on bunions I'd acquired in 1968 wearing plastic shoes as a waitress at Kip's Big Boy and on my preference for flimsy high heels. I'd logged in years of hospital nursing that required many hours navigating long hallways on hard floors, and I assumed that that kind of abuse would naturally take a toll.

Always on a quest to find a comfortable pair of shoes, I blamed chilblains, corns, and calluses as the reason for my discomfort. For most of my forties and early fifties I settled on the cause as a combination of bad shoes, bad habits, and possibly bad genes. I took it all in stride.

One of the hazards of a career in the medical profession is the tendency to self-diagnose. In 1971, as a young nursing student, I'd fallen prey to this pitfall. One morning I woke up with a painless Ping-Pong ball sized lump on my neck. Convinced I had lymphoma, I spent several sleepless nights worrying about my mortality. The fact that my grandmother died of this disease in 1962 gave credence to my diagnosis, and I even called my new boyfriend, Tom, to tell him of my imminent demise. Suffice it to say, I was subsequently found to have mononucleosis, a common virus, and the lump disappeared.

But when I stepped out of the shower one day in my fifty-fourth year and felt my foot go numb, I was long past this suggestible stage. I'd had a similar sensation while standing at the checkout counter of the grocery store earlier in the week, but I had dismissed it as a fluke. *It's probably a pinched nerve. Too much heavy lifting during our recent move. Yet another sign of old age. What else is new?* I mentioned the problem to my husband, and he voiced the same opinion. True to form, we both agreed on a liberal application of "wait and see" or as my husband likes to say "live long enough to get over it."

To be honest, I'd experienced other strange symptoms in my legs and feet for years. Coming home after long walks, I sometimes detected spasms in my calves and thighs. After climbing a tower on the Oregon Coast ten years earlier, I remember that my legs felt like twitching mush. It was a long climb, I reasoned, trying to brush away my concern. I quickly attributed the bothersome symptoms to being out of shape.

Things suddenly got much worse on the morning I accompanied my husband to a surgical center for his hernia repair. I've never been one to sit for very long and had been pacing for several hours—the surgery was taking much longer than I'd expected. Without warning, a creeping numbness beginning in both feet spread to mid-thigh and then to my waist. Something was seriously wrong.

My husband and I both walked slowly out to the parking lot after his release from the medical facility—Tom hobbled by his surgical incision and his wife by strange sensations in the lower half of her body. I waited to reveal what was happening until we got to the car. We quickly discussed all kinds of serious possibilities: Guillain-Barré (an ascending numbness and paralysis caused by an autoimmune response after a viral illness), a brain or spinal tumor, multiple sclerosis. None of these were good. We took advantage of Tom's medical connections, and I saw the doctor that afternoon.

Over the coming weeks there would be neurological tests, blood work, a spinal tap, and an MRI. Doctors deemed the

MRI inconclusive; the spinal tap showed oligoclonal banding consistent with the diagnosis of multiple sclerosis. The neurologist phoned, and it became official. I'd moved from being healthy into the world of chronic illness.

Many years later, my symptoms remain sensory, and for this reason I'm currently considered to have the mildest form of the disease. Quick diagnosis and early treatment with one of the new designer drugs may have helped; damage to the myelin coating surrounding my nerves has been mostly held in check. Like my daughter, Natalie, I may be exquisitely sensitive to these medications. The destruction progresses very slowly and I don't know why.

I suffer from burning feet and legs and an occasional strange pervasive feeling that something is not right, which is mildly troubling. Fleeting visual problems have posed no lasting threat to my vision. The major impact on my life has been pain on days I do too much. I rarely walk for long distances anymore. Activity seems to exacerbate my condition. The car has become a necessary tool to preserve the quality of my life, and I now tootle back and forth from car to house much as my grandmother did. Of course, I know this level of function could change without notice. That's the nature of MS.

For now, the move from health to chronic illness has been mostly a conceptual one. The Kübler-Ross stages of grief that come with this type of change (denial, anger, depression, grief, and acceptance) have yet to hit. Perhaps this is because my symptoms have been so mild or because I'm older and expect to slow down and not feel as well as I did in my youth. Perhaps it's because I've followed the path of illness with so many of my patients and friends always asking myself: *Why them?* Now that it's my turn, I don't ask, *Why me?* I ask, *Why not?*

I have known many MS patients who have much more of a challenge. One very precious friend, who has had MS since she was nine, told me: "I accept what comes. What else can I do?" She uses her chin to move her electric wheelchair and her eyes to send emails. She enjoys the ocean surf with the aid of adaptive equipment, and she rides her horse. Thanks to special programs where she lives, she's even been skydiving. She parents a teenage daughter. Her courage and immense spirit refuse to let a disease define who she is.

But at times I miss my old body and rue the years I spent hating it. I miss feeling whole and good. I hold my grandchildren and think how they will never know me as I once was—healthy and bustling down the hallways of a busy medical-surgical ward, thriving on doing, moving with ease, feeling good. They will always know a dowdy old woman with wrinkles and a double chin, who lumbers across the room with increasing effort, tottering on swollen painful legs that feel like rotting stumps because she's not well. I've come full circle to taste the bitterness of my own illness—the nurse as patient, a work in progress trying to learn how to live on the other side of medicine. And yet I hope for better things to come.

As a young child and teenager I remember how excited I was to sleep in a tent at Blue Bay Girl Scout Camp in the Hamptons. My family would pack all the gear in our red and white 57 Studebaker station wagon and drive out on Long Island to a special place where the forest meets that ocean–the air infused with the smells of sea weed and pine. It was such a treat to get away from the city. The sandy floors of the tent and the mosquitoes and dirt didn't bother me at all. I never wanted to go home!

My enthusiasm for the tent camping changed when I got older. Although I still enjoy nature, I can only take it for so long before the bugs and dirt start to get to me. Sleeping in a tent is more uncomfortable and less fun. I'm much less willing to sign up for an outdoor trip that might involve really cold nights, rain dripping overhead through sodden canvas, and wet bedding. I find that I'm less tolerant of "camper's hair" in the morning and the lumps and bumps under my sleeping bag.

So it is with our bodies. With each passing year we may find that living in these tents of ours can be harder than the year before. Aches and pains set in, diseases and health problems make life harder and more uncomfortable

Of course we try to fix our tents. Hospitals are full of people who are having their body parts replaced, removed, or readjusted. As you read these words, hearts, hernias, and hemorrhoids are all being retooled. Hips and knees are routinely replaced. Doctors are in the business of making repairs on the human body. They are modern day "tent menders," but they have their limits. Like some of our family tents that got blown on to the highway by a dust-devil during a swim meet, repairs can't always be made. As everyone knows, even the most modern medicine can't always fix what's broken.

Over the years I can remember many stories that I've read in books by Joni Eareckson Tada, but one of the most memorable tells about a man named Steve Coyle. Steve was an active young man in the prime of his life who loved to swim and walk on the beach. One day he had an accident that left him permanently paralyzed. He lived as a quadriplegic, dependent on others for help with his daily needs and a few years later developed cancer. Although he was only 27 years old his tent was collapsing.

Steve wrote a poem about asking God for healing. In it he regrets the hubris of youth that led him to take his tent for granted. He asks his maker to restore his sagging canvas and broken poles. He prays to God. The answer God gives him is explained in a Bible verse in 2 Corinthians 4:16 NIV and is full of hope.

> *...though outwardly we are wasting away, yet inwardly we are being renewed day by day. For our light and momentary troubles are achieving for us an eternal glory that far outweighs them all. So we fix our eyes not on what is seen, but on what is unseen. For what is seen is temporary, but what is unseen is eternal.*

These are the last lines of a poem written by Steve Coyle.

Please don't grieve over some old tent,
Old canvas walls that have been spent
For a mansion that has been built by Me
Will last you for eternity.

Joni writes: "With that assurance, Steve Coyle gladly broke camp and moved on".

Chapter 21

❦

An Impacted Life

*Sometimes good things fall apart so
better things can fall together.*

Marilyn Monroe

I was a twenty-year-old college student when I first realized I had wisdom teeth. Angry gums and unrelenting pain ultimately led me to the wrenching conclusion that my budding molars would have to go. It was 1968, and as a naive college freshman, I turned to the phone book to look for a dentist.

The office of my new doctor, packed into a storefront downtown, offered a tiny waiting room that reeked of curry and marijuana. Two sagging couches draped in madras sat in one corner surrounded by an assortment of potted plants molting onto a scruffy tile floor. The receptionist ushered me into the back room through beaded curtains, and I found myself reclining on a leatherette chaise lounge staring at a funky collage of album covers that papered the ceiling.

As I reclined on cool Naugahyde contemplating my fate, a ponytailed dentist placed a small mask over my nose and mouth, and I surrendered to the harrowing but necessary ordeal of having four teeth pulled. Thanks to nitrous oxide, I don't remember the pain. This happened in the late 60's. The Age of Aquarius was dawning. Sadly for me, it took four impacted wisdom teeth to finally "get trippin'."

But there was no sweet relief in 1989 when I found myself facing the prospect of what could be termed an "impacted life." Craving a more rural type of medicine and lured by hospital recruiters eager to find a family practice physician, my adventure loving husband saw an opportunity he couldn't pass up. One hot August night, Tom announced his plans to move our family to a tiny isolated town in the Eastern Oregon desert. Many serious discussions and tearful evenings ensued, but, in the end, I relented to help my husband realize his dream. With a heavy heart, this former New Yorker agreed to relocate to a small desert town in the middle of nowhere.

The town of Lakeview is located in the center of cattle country, euphemistically called the Oregon Outback. This is a land where giant alkaline ponds smell of rotting brine shrimp, coyotes eat stray dogs, and mayflies buzz with abandon. Harsh dust storms billow in the stifling hot summer air, and whiteouts obliterate frosted winter landscapes. Mosquitoes in clouds as thick as custard have been known to infuse the sky, coating skin, hair, and glasses and rendering the air unbreathable. Leeches lurk in shallow swimming holes resplendent with blooms of algae. Locusts swoop in swarms. Contrary to its moniker, there's no lake in view.

One hundred miles of sagebrush and juniper stretch between L-town (as it is fondly called) and the nearest larger community to the west and it's two hundred miles to real civilization in all other directions. As the only town of any size in a county that's bigger than the state of Connecticut, the population has held steady at about 2,500 since the early 1900s. Blisteringly cold winters with treacherous road conditions and long drives to anywhere are some of the things that have kept the place from growing.

Lake County also has the reputation of being radioactive,

a holdover from rumors and a few old news stories about contamination left by the Lucky Lass and White King uranium mining operations during the 1950s and 1960s. The cleanup was completed in 1999, but Lakeview's old reputation continued to glow. Upon learning of our planned move, friends kidded us about "blushing fluorescent" and setting off airport screening devices. I failed to see the humor.

In fact, I failed to see anything positive about my exile to the Oregon Outback. Having grown up on Long Island, I craved the excitement and the opportunities afforded by proximity to a city. Although mothering was my primary job at the time, I still secretly hoped to have a career, and a sleepy cow town hundreds of miles from nowhere seemed the last place I could make my dreams a reality. Doctors' wives generally do not fit in as nurses in small rural hospitals, and those who try this route often face insurmountable resentment from staff and complaints of nepotism. *What could I possibly do there?* Even nature seemed so blatantly inhospitable that I felt as if I had been exiled to Afghanistan or some similarly windswept, desolate terrain with few prospects for any kind of satisfying life.

As the move approached, my heart sank, sucked down into an imaginary quagmire of quicksand like an unfortunate cowhand in an old western. Even my body forged a protest— every joint froze with the sudden onset of fibromyalgia, a sort of somatic headache that mirrored my psychological suffering. My sleep became restless, and at times I could barely move. When I imagined the stultifying life ahead, I pictured chronic ennui. I saw myself aging before my time, sunbaked in the dusty high desert air, my spirit drying up and slowly tumbling across the arid landscape to the tune of "Happy Trails." On one of our first visits, the windshield became obliterated by the yellow goo of the thousands of desert locusts swarming to premature death. My future looked just as bleak. *Where's the hippy dentist when you need him?*

A nearly thirty-foot tall bowlegged cowboy greeted us as

we drove into town that first day, towing our U-Haul. Tex, also known as Tall Man, only added to my despair. A sinister-looking cowboy with a sneering grin, barely-noticeable Texas tie, rumpled black fedora, battered boots, and a gun belt slung low on his hips, Tex had been greeting visitors for fifty years, standing guard with his six shooter pointed upward to welcome (or was it to warn?) all who ventured into town past the claptrap yards leading to L-town central. Was it my imagination that the townspeople seemed just as sinister and unwelcoming?

It would be some time before I understood that a steady stream of innocent wives accompanying their frontier-seeking husbands filed through Lakeview every year only to move within months of discovering that a drive to the nearest Costco was a seven-hour round trip by car. People were slow to offer their affections to newcomers who more often than not were just a flicker on the social landscape. Five years into my own residency, I found myself remarking to my husband after a party to welcome a new newspaper editor and his wife, "I'll give her six months." To no one's surprise, she was gone in two.

Considering the initial impressions that clouded my attitude, it's a wonder that I didn't join the ranks of the short-timers. But I stayed. Over twenty years later I look back and consider staying in Lakeview as one of the best things I ever did.

Lakeview's isolation and small population have resulted in a homogeny of community that is seldom found in other places. Distinctions of social background, education, and position hold little sway. "There really is no social hierarchy here," remarked one long-term resident, "although a few persist in trying."

Look around the gym during a high school basketball game and one will soon realize a personal connection with almost everyone there. The guard's mother cleaned your teeth. The center's grandpa had a dog that bit you in the leg while you were riding your bicycle. The coach once stopped to help you fix a flat.

Living in Lakeview, it's impossible to not know that poverty in America is real and that everyone has problems. Because there is so little happening, news travels across town with the speed of light. A friend visiting from Houston was stunned to walk downtown and be greeted by name by the grocer, the baker, and even the town librarian. Rumors raged. A woman fainted on Main Street in front of the library and word of "a drive-by shooting" dispersed through town like feathers in the wind.

Lakeview was once featured in a book called *The Kindness of Strangers*: *Penniless across America*, chronicling the experiences of the author, Mike McIntyre, as he hitchhiked across America without money. A stop in Lakeview included stories of the author's encounters with a man named Tim, who provided a meal and a tent, and Mike in a white pickup, who helped with a coat. Although only first names were used in the book, everyone in Lakeview knew who these men were: Mike, a local painter, and Tim, who lived on Main Street with his four children.

The slower pace and intimate nature of life in Lakeview provided numerous chances to forge relationships. Because of the town's remote location and the interdependencies that resulted, many of Lakeview's small town attributes seemed exaggerated. To relay the depth of life lived in this small isolated community, I punt to a description of the iconoclastic institutions immortalized by the fictional residents of Mayberry: the beauty salon and the barber shop.

In the early 1980s I brought my son Neal to a barber in St. Maries, Idaho, for his first haircut. The small town shop, with its requisite barber pole, ancient pump-up chairs, floating combs, and jars of colored tonic, was a small dark establishment in the center of Main Street smelling of old wood and smoke. The barber chairs looked like something from a tintype in the early1900s. I fully expected to see Andy Griffith or Barney Fife reclining lathered for a shave, or sitting on the plastic-covered metal furniture reading *Field & Stream* in the deep recesses of the decidedly-male establishment.

As a mother, I'd looked forward to this rite of passage conducted in a bastion of male bonding, but I soon found that coaxing a two-year-old boy into a styling chair is no easy task. The barber in his high-collared white tunic, the antiseptic-looking seat, and the assortment of sharp metal tools all evoked memories of unpleasant experiences involving invasive procedures endured elsewhere. The barber greeted us at the door looking less than elated at the prospect of dealing with a balky customer and his mop of blonde curls.

Barber Tuttle stood back and rocked with impatience as I spouted reassuring words and eventually cajoled my child into the booster seat. To my horror, Tuttle pointed to one of the many cylinders that lined his counter. It contained what appeared to be a stack of plastic human ears in various shapes and sizes floating in an iridescent blue liquid. He leaned over Neal, his scissors clicking, and brusquely admonished his little patron to sit still at the risk of leaving the shop looking like Vincent Van Gogh. Trips to the barber were never easy after that.

When Neal was six we began going to a barber named Shube, who practiced his craft in a narrow shop in L-town central. Shube might have been five feet four inches tall in his prime before age compacted his vertebrae and stooped his tiny frame to less than five feet. Ninety years old and counting, he'd spent untold hours hunched over his customers for more than seven decades. With his colored polyester smock, meticulously-coifed tuft of thick snowy hair, and a one-hundred-pound frame, he had the appearance of an elfin dentist.

Shube worked diligently without much chit chat. His haircuts were never quick affairs. A careful snipping, clipping, and dusting often took the good part of an hour—a lesson in patience. Like the immaculate lawn in front of his bachelor pad by the grammar school, his work proved meticulous, not a follicle out of line.

Trips to Shube became history when Neal turned twelve. The decision to self-clip was made after the fateful day that the elf-like stylist made a slip with his clippers. Hair tattoos were popular at the time, and my son requested an "S," for swimming, carved in his hair on the back of his head. The elderly barber took his time, unfortunately looking into the mirror as he worked. After half an hour he finally spun the chair around to reveal the results of his painstaking labor—a perfect backwards "S" in the back of my son's head—a sort of question mark for all to see. Neal's hair would grow and eventually erase the question mark but not the damaged to his pride. This event had symbolic meaning, bringing to mind Neal's initial reticence about climbing into the barber chair years ago. He still had both his ears, but trust is something that is hard to fix once it's broken.

Anytime one sits in a chair and offers his or her head of hair to the creative whims of a scissor-wielding artist, there is an element of trust. An acute understanding of this very real risk also becomes painfully evident for patrons of a small town beauty parlor.

Beauty salons have long been female centers for congenial conversation, companionship, and community building. Although I wore my hair long and straight during my hippy years in the 1960s and 1970s, there came a day after the birth of my second child when I decided to have a haircut.

Once a woman enters the small town styling system, there is almost no turning back. One bad cut, style, or perm leads to another, and, as the years pass, it soon becomes evident that several weeks of one's total lifespan have been spent wearing a large bib with feet dangling in a chair two feet off the floor. This is time endured for the sake of appearances in the quest to be, if not beautiful, at least socially acceptable. Of course, as beauty wanes with age, it seems like the trips to these establishments become more frequent and more urgent. The short helmet hair styles favored by older women need upkeep, and, overnight, one finds oneself addicted.

Some small town mavens avoid local salons like the plague. It's too hard to put trust in someone you know so well with something so personal as your appearance. It's too hard to make oneself that vulnerable. A death in the family, a messy divorce, or the stylist's dislike for your brother can render her cut as uneven as her emotional state. One beautician with a history of family tragedies was accused of raking the comb across patrons' heads in anguish. Stories of her alleged scalp wounds continue as the fodder of rumor. Another was known for her lopsided styling. Sometimes it is easier to trust a stranger.

Small town salon banter is all about what is happening locally. Some tidbits of news heard in the stylist's chair are hard to hear, even with a nursing background. I would have just as soon not known: the details of Ethel's childbirth experience, Marge's hysterectomy, or what Jack the undertaker found in a client's pocket. Some people avoid these establishments to avoid the gossip, but I've heard that beauty parlor talk can be considered to be a form of prayer. Even so, for some it was just too much information.

When I look back on my small town hair styling experiences, I don't remember the hairstyles I got, or even the scuttlebutt. What I do remember is that it was at the beauty parlor where I was able to comfort a hairdresser who, grieving the death of her daughter-in-law in a tragic accident, began to cry into a towel she had just used to dry my hair. The salon was where I saw young girls gather around a very elderly Minnie, waiting for her to style them for their weddings and proms. It was there that the stylist loaned me the two purple topiaries and swags adorning her shop for me to use at a friend's wedding. It was there I got to know a special man named Shube, whose haircuts were his art.

The barber chair is a metaphor for letting go of ego, pride, and even fear, and embracing what is better—knowing and being known. This is at the crux of small town life. Lakeview taught me the value of that kind of community.

In his book *Spiritual Notes to Myself*, Hugh Prather describes this kind of living:

"We are walking in a ticker tape parade. That's all that's going on. Some pieces of confetti read 'great calves,' some 'chronic sinus,' some 'no noticeable hair loss,' some 'multiple sclerosis'. . . . Don't judge your neighbor by what pieces fall on his or her shoulder."

I can't think of a better description of small town life.

Tex still stands in front of the one and only Safeway in the county. He was retired as greeter at both ends of town in the early 1990s, replaced by a more contemporary cowboy with stylish hair peeking from a too-big hat. The new guy, dubbed Rex, looks more like the cowboy wannabes from the city sporting a handlebar mustache, red neckerchief, shiny boots, and a massive belt buckle. The gun is gone. Even before *Brokeback Mountain*, Rex's stance, with one leg bent, one hand on his hip, and the other behind his back, led locals to nickname him the Fey Cowboy. It's a change that didn't sit well with the many conservative ranch folks and rodeo aficionados. Fey is no John Wayne, and yet he welcomes.

We moved away in 2004 but returned to visit friends in Lakeview several years later, and Rex *aka* Fey, greeted us as we drove into town. It was good to see him. Although we'd been gone for some time, the people we met still treated us like family. Suddenly thrust back into life where everyone knows your name, we were stunned by the number and variety of people who remembered us for the oddest of reasons. "You brought me a case of water when my daughter was diagnosed with cancer," one woman remarked. "You woke us up at midnight to get gas, when your son had a head injury," said another. One woman mentioned that I once put a Band-Aid on her finger.

Yes, this born and bred Yankee moved to Lakeview and learned to like it. For fifteen years, Tex and Rex greeted us more times than I care to remember. The sucking leeches, the locust goo, the snowy whiteouts and silty dust-outs, the mosquito body stockings, and the rancid stench of briny lakes all became part of life. Mayflies made us mad. The wind whipped us senseless, and dust devils took our tents. In the highest town in Oregon, we sometimes found ourselves immobile in a muffled world of windswept snow. We spent weeks, maybe months, sitting in our car on mind and bottom numbing trips to maintain contact with civilization. And one summer our beloved dog disappeared in the sage-packed desert, presumably breakfast for a pack of hungry coyotes.

There are so many things that happen in life that can never be seen as wholly good. Disease, death, tragedy, and disappointment happen and are often beyond our power to prevent them. Decisions made in haste or even after careful thought can lead us to places we'd rather not have gone— misguided careers that don't fit, misconceived ideas doomed to folly, miserable relationships that only add to life's troubles, or hard circumstances that we never anticipated. I've often thought that my choice of a career in nursing was one such misstep that consumed a good chunk of my youth and cost me the opportunity for more satisfying pursuits. But no longer. With a different set of eyes, I see nursing as a gift that infused my life with rich experience and insight.

The opportunity to live for over a decade and a half in the tiny desert town of Lakeview was also one such gift. It was there that I saw what seemed to be one of the worst things that could ever happen turn into one of the best. Painful interludes fade to gray in contrast to the brilliant kaleidoscope of life lived in relationship. When I eventually dug myself out of the mire, I found that what I thought was sucking quicksand that would trap me solid in the wastelands of a chalky desert was actually an amazing opportunity to experience life more fully, in brilliant color, with an intensity that sparkled like I hadn't imagined possible. What I'd first viewed as an impacted life became a life impacted. And like my experience in the dentist chair decades earlier, it was a high I never expected.

Chapter 22

✠

Marshmallows Don't Satisfy

> *"We want something else which can hardly be put into words—to be united with the beauty we see, to pass into it, to receive it into ourselves, to bathe in it, to become part of it."*

The Weight of Glory
C.S. Lewis

On a cool rainy evening three weeks before Christmas, my husband and I drove over the mountains to watch our niece's children perform in their school's Winter Extravaganza. This special event, replacing the traditional Christmas concert, was being held in the elementary school gymnasium in a medium-sized town near Seattle where they live. As we trudged through the dark and misty parking lot and filed into the building, I heard a familiar holiday tune coming from the gym: "It's a Marshmallow World." This harsh pop music blasted through speakers on the floor as our little family hustled to take our seats.

Tom and I weren't surprised that the title of the public school event had been changed. We'd become used to "Merry Christmas" being replaced with less innocuous greetings like

"Happy Holidays" and "Sunny Solstice." As our culture places more and more emphasis on being politically correct, religious sentiment in the public square is deemed irrelevant by many and offensive by some.

But as we marched into the huge gym and headed for the bleachers that night, my mind filled with memories of a concert held many decades earlier on a magical night in December 1958. The grounds of my school in Floral Park were covered with several feet of snow. People garbed in holiday finery scurried with anticipation to find their seats in our school's turn-of-the-century auditorium glittering with tinsel and trim. Dark oak walls were adorned with conifer wreaths and festive garlands, which infused the air with the fragrance of balsam and pine. Large green and red bulbs glowed on stage as heavy velvet curtains parted to reveal my second grade class dressed in homemade cherry-red elf costumes for a performance of the play *Elvis and the Shoemaker* and a chorus of Christmas carols. Young voices rose, the familiar melodies of "Away in a Manger," "O Little Town of Bethlehem," and "Silent Night" ringing upward to the heavens. The acoustics were *par excellence*. The music comforted and moved.

I waxed nostalgic for that evening of my childhood as I sat on a hard bench with my middle-aged knees against a stranger's back under caged fluorescent lights in a giant gym. The tiered bleachers were packed. There were no decorations. The unmistakable odors of sweat and rubber filled the atmosphere.

Restless children, dressed in a wide assortment of styles ranging from lacy dresses to camouflage sweat suits, stood against the gray, plastic tumbling mats that lined the walls, to wait with their pacing teachers. One by one the principal called each class to stand in uneven rows along red and blue lines on the glossy mustard-colored floor in the center of the gym. The children performed songs about candy, presents, and snowmen, all set to the tunes of such classics as "Twinkle, Twinkle, Little

Star," "Row, Row, Row Your Boat," and "The Farmer in the Dell." Their juvenile voices rose and quickly dissipated into the mammoth room.

I sat there that night with my boomer heart longing for the substance of Christmas concerts of yesteryear–pining for the time when Christmas was more than a winter break and music was more than jingles about Toyland and the whipped cream world of snow. I ached for the concerts of my youth when children sang about love and peace and joy that knows no earthly comparison...when young voices lifted in praise of a higher calling.

As the concert ended and families reunited to shuffle out to the parking lot through the school cafeteria, no one in the crowd seemed particularly happy. With minds full of the fluff of pop culture and banal ditties humming in our heads, we headed into the dreary night to resume our lives. The performances were a tribute to the material world. They rang as hollow as the massive empty gymnasium that we'd just left. The evening proved memorable for all the wrong reasons. It brought to mind an aching loneliness, a need for something more—the need that is at the heart of so many lives of quiet desperation.

Marshmallows just don't satisfy.

There came a time when I realized my need for more than the junk food of secular morality. For years I'd stepped up to the spiritual salad bar to sample its offerings, only to leave wholly unsatisfied. Like many people, I'd searched for a personal version of spirituality and what's trendily considered a more "authentic" life. The New Age buffet, in perpetual flux, was a perfect fit for my independent personality. I once believed in personal choice and tolerance—whatever floats your boat. My ears always itched to hear something new.

With so many variations on the spiritual theme, I soon found I could fashion my beliefs to suit, rounding off the Four Agreements, the Eightfold Path, and the Ten Perfections, with a blend of astrology, yoga, and Indian pantheistic wisdom to taste. I added a dollop of Buddhism, Oprah's Eckhart Tolle, spiritual guru Wayne Dyer, and a sprinkling of poetry by the thirteenth century poet Rumi to make my custom product. With a few sentimental family hymns and a passing nod to the wisdom of the prophet Jesus thrown in for old time's sake, I had my religion. This individualized, stylized faith discounted traditions and the amazing truths and supreme validity of the scriptures found in the Holy Bible—an ancient text that's instructed and comforted through the ages and helped countless people to know God.

I was forty years old when my life experiences came together and spurred me on to turn back to the religion of my youth. I reopened the Bible, and the words of the Sermon on the Mount seemed to pop. I saw the Old Testament stories that so troubled me as a youngster as an anthropological study of the human condition. I moved my gaze from Christians and political Christianity to the person of Jesus through the Bible. The God I met there was nothing like the one I had known in catechism class. I met Him in what some might think as the most unlikely of places—through the love of a young teenager in a motorized wheelchair.

I met God at disability camp.

Chapter 23

Joni

It's July 1967, and my best friend, Alice Hwang, and I are riding in the back seat of her brother Shu-mei's car, driving down Jericho Turnpike in Queens on our way to the pool. I'm seventeen and about to start my senior year in high school. The radio's playing Dylan's "Mr. Tambourine Man," and we're reveling in our teenage freedom. Like so many Long Island summer days the air's heavy with humidity. I crank the car window down and turn my head towards the sky. The winds of promise hit my face. I'm drunk, but not on booze. I'm full of youthful enthusiasm and lofty expectations. "And what wine is so sparkling, what so fragrant, what so intoxicating, as possibility!" says Søren Kierkegaard. On this particular day I'm blotto.

I'm looking forward to college. Hopes of applying to Swathmore or Columbia consume my waking thoughts. As my friends and I speed down the busy street, I'm blissfully unaware that I'll soon be forced to recreate my vision. In a mere three months my parents will announce plans to move our family West taking me away from Long Island and the aunts, uncles, grandparents, and friends of my childhood–ruining my senior year and dashing all hopes for an Ivy League education. I'm still unaware that the New York Regents diploma I've been working toward for years will slip away from me and never materialize and that options I think secure will vaporize, replaced with culture shock and boredom in the wastelands of east Texas. The move will change my view of what's possible, take me to places I don't want to go, and bring experiences beyond my adolescent imagination.

But on that summer afternoon in the car, I remain oblivious to the tenuous hold I have on my future. Heady with budding freedom and the invincibility of my age, all my thoughts are sunny and naïve. Nebulous hopes of doing something *great* hibernate in the nether regions of my brain. The drug metaphors of Dylan's lyrics blaring through the car speakers go over my head. A single line of the song is all I hear: "I'm ready to go anywhere." Little do I know.

Many miles away, somewhere on Chesapeake Bay on what is possibly the very same hot July afternoon in 1967, another seventeen-year-old girl with big dreams is sunning herself on a raft. She's laughing with her sister and friends, reveling in her teenage independence, and also full of plans for a lifetime ahead. She too looks forward to the future and daydreams of greatness. She's even prayed about it.

Standing on the raft ready to dive, this beautiful, tanned, and taut young girl is also unaware of the changes that are about to come her way and take her to places she would rather not go—to experiences she never imagined. She lifts her arms to dive and, seconds later, her head hits sand in too-shallow water breaking her neck. In an instant she is permanently paralyzed from the shoulders down. This girl, Joni Eareckson Tada, will spend the rest of her life in a wheelchair.

Like my patient in nursing school, Joni finds herself pinned to a Stryker frame with a broken spine and too much time to think. She knows a season of despair, feels even suicidal, but eventually, in spite of her life-changing injury, comes to see a vision for the days ahead. Before her accident, Joni asked God to use her life. He will prove faithful.

* * * * * * *

Despite my initial grief about my parent's move I eventually learned to love the West. The upheaval that moving to Texas brought was hard at first, but I adjusted and went on to the ordinary activities of an average life. It was Joni's life that proved extraordinary and soared far above the mundane.

The changes that Joni's accident brought could only be described as devastating and took immense courage, but she rose to the challenge. As a renowned artist, radio personality, and author of over fifty books, she would be the one who went on to do something *great*—something *really great*. Her strong faith in God led her to start a Christian ministry called *Joni and Friends* (JAF) that has touched millions worldwide, supporting, caring for, and nurturing people affected by disability. At some point, over thirty years from that day in July 1967, our lives touched.

As a new Christian in 1999, sensing a need to spend time with my then fourteen-year-old daughter Noelle, I searched the internet for a short-term service project that we could do together. It may seem strange, but the experience at the bedside of my paralyzed patient in nursing school in 1971 still gnawed at my psyche. Troubling thoughts about the capricious nature of suffering still bothered me. A lot of baggage remained unpacked.

I had been moving toward Christianity ever since I heard a pastor named Don White talk at a Toastmasters club meeting in Lakeview, and, somehow, a Christian disability camp seemed the place to look my feelings squarely in the face. During my years as an overworked nurse, I'd buried a lot of troubling emotions, and I knew I needed to dig deep to deal with them. I clicked on the *Joni and Friends* ministry website as a way to take on these demons, and downloaded two applications.

Noelle and I signed up to be short-term missionaries (STMs)

at a JAF Family Camp for a week. Our aim was to help families affected by disability have fun at a retreat site in the California Redwoods near Santa Cruz. No hands-on nursing care would be required; personal needs would be addressed by family or caregivers. The goal was to help the person with a disability and their family feel loved and accepted and to have a good time at a camp in a beautiful setting. Life can be hard when you are disabled or responsible for someone's care all day every day. When it comes to serious disabilities like autism, paralysis, and severe cerebral palsy, parents and other caregivers often feel isolated and overwhelmed.

Essentially clueless about the ramifications of what we'd agreed to, I didn't have answers to my young daughter's questions. "Will we be taking care of people with mental disabilities?" she asked with some trepidation as we drove down the highway toward California. As a nurse, I was used to caring for all types of people, and the prospect of what my daughter termed "mental disabilities" didn't worry me. The trip into the alien territory that is California seemed much more daunting. But camp would prove the shallow nature of my knowledge. I would quickly discover that I didn't understand the meaning of the word "disability."

As soon as we arrived and began Short Term Missionary (STM) orientation, I learned that the number and variety of disabilities affecting the campers would prove to be far beyond the scope of my experience as a registered nurse. Many genetic syndromes, including that of my charge that year, hadn't been covered in nursing school. On the first day at camp, we were given a brief description of our assignments including the disabled person's abilities and preferences and a short course on autism, blindness, deafness, and wheelchair etiquette. On the second day we were set loose with instructions to love.

As STMs we would spend the week caring for families with the aim of doing whatever it took to help everyone enjoy camp. Sometimes that meant pushing a child on a swing for hours on end, helping a blind woman explore the gift shop, or playing cards all afternoon with a group of women in wheelchairs. Sometimes it meant running after campers and missing dinner or, as it did for my daughter the first year, jumping off the diving board over a hundred times a day.

Soon after the families arrived, a young camper in a motorized chair approached me near the central lawn. "What's your disability?" he asked earnestly. I had yet to be diagnosed with MS, and I had to admit at the time that most of mine didn't show. I blurted out a few problems off the top of my head: slight myopia, a tendency to be impatient, poor math skills. In truth, I had too many hidden disabilities to enumerate ad lib. I was supposed to be the missionary—the one doing the helping. The boy, named Bryce, looked at me and through me. Something moved.

Remembered scenes from my twelve years at Joni and Friends (JAF) Family Retreats meld together into a whirling collection of epiphanies and relationships so rich and special that I cherish each one of them with all my being. Each and every person I've met at these camps, visibly disabled or not, had something to teach me about life and love and the power of the spirit that comes through no matter how profound the disability. Bryce and many other people I met at JAF camps over the years showed me Christ

As a volunteer at JAF, I've had the opportunity to gain a glimpse into the world of a woman who's been blind since birth, grown to know a wonderful couple, who, after the husband's permanent paralysis from a fall off a ladder, embraced the future with tremendous grace and dignity. Special people with multiple sclerosis have touched me with their immense courage, facing each day as the nerve connections so many of us take for granted, slowly short circuit and take their independence. Parents of children with severe autism, genetic syndromes, and devastating birth defects have blessed me beyond measure as they've shown their dedicated commitment and unconditional love in the face of difficult issues and what can seem like overwhelming responsibilities. Knowing and loving their children and seeing God work through them—this has been my tremendous privilege.

Betty stands out as a woman full of love and joy. She woke one morning to find that she was slowly losing control of her body. After weeks of tests, doctors were still unsure of what caused her condition. Over time, the creeping numbness and loss of function slowed and seemed to stabilize, but not before Betty lost her ability to walk and found herself unable to care for herself or her family. Her husband divorced her. She moved to a nursing home and tried to cope with the serious deficits in her cognitive abilities and severely-impaired mobility that resulted from her illness. Despite the fact that she faced the loss of all she held dear, Betty glowed. She gave effusive thanks for little things, like a successful trip to the bathroom, and she often sang in gratitude for even the tiniest gifts with arms stretched upward. I stood by her chair as her short-term missionary in awe of her joy, basking in a light that seemed to come from out of this world.

It's a tradition for the short-term missionaries to sing "The Servant Song" to families on the first day of camp, and every time we do my heart swells with humility. The very words of this song remind me of Florence Nightingale and an old story about one of her patients, who, when looking up to her as she cared for him on his bed, saw the image of Christ.

> *I will hold the Christ-light for you,*
> *In the night time of your fear,*

But it's the final lines of that song that stunned me the first time I heard them. They continue to stun me to this day:

> *Pray that I may I have the grace*
> *To let you be my servant too.*

And so it was that I learned one of the secrets of the Joni and Friends Family Retreat: "God has chosen the foolish things of the world to shame the wise. God has chosen the weak things of the world to shame the things which are strong" (1 Corinthians 1:27 NIV). His power is perfected in weakness.

I discovered there that we all have disabilities, although often many of the them don't show. I thought I went to camp to help to the disabled, but it turns out that they ministered to me.

Close to 35 years after that afternoon when I stood at the bedside of my paralyzed patient, I finally met Joni Eareckson Tada. She was sitting on a wooden deck under the redwoods surrounded by friends and well-wishers during one of the Family Camps in California. In her characteristically gracious manner, she greeted me with a smile and noted something we had in common. I was wearing a jumper with the label of her designer friend, Carol Anderson. I leaned over her wheelchair and someone took our picture. We exchanged a few words, nothing serious. Joni periodically shows up at these camps now and again, and, as an international celebrity, her attention is always in high demand.

I never had a chance to really talk with Joni—to tell her about my experience with the paralyzed patient back in nursing school and how it bothered me. I never had the opportunity to share how that single moment at my patient's bedside eventually led me to JAF camp and later to a deeper relationship with Christ. I never had the occasion to explain the tremendous change that JAF Family Retreats made in my life.

On that day at camp, as the short term missionaries lined up in the central aisle of the sanctuary to have their servant hands blessed before the campers arrived that afternoon, I saw Joni sitting in her motorized wheelchair by the altar—her husband, Ken, at her side. I wasn't expecting it, but suddenly I was overcome with emotion. The immensity of Joni's suffering for those thirty-some years since the accident in 1967 and our parallel lives, so different in so many ways, hit me with full force. The blessings I so easily take for granted—my privacy, the ability to feel my body, walk, turn over in bed, and use my hands—had all been denied Joni for almost four decades.

I wept for Joni and the pain she had endured. I was overcome with awe and gratitude for all the good that had come out of her suffering—the camps, the over 25,000 wheelchairs distributed to disadvantaged disabled people worldwide, her books, and the comfort and inspiration for all those affected by disability. Countless people have been blessed.

As I quietly sobbed in the arms of my husband, years of pent-up emotions flowed. Tears poured for all the patients I'd never cried for, for all the pain that I hoped would be redeemed as Joni's had been through her faith in a loving God—the God who the Bible tells us "makes all things beautiful in his time" (Ecclesiastes 3:11 NIV).

Chapter 24

Peace

Memories pour
They're flooding past.
Regrets and plans...
Life went too fast
Whelming grief
Comes bearing down.
In torrents deep
I fear I'll drown.

Excerpt from *Johnny*
A poem by Janet Richards

I've heard that most people can remember the fine details of particular moments when they got very bad news—what was happening when the policeman came to the door, the phone rang at three a.m., or they heard of the horror of September 11, 2001. When the news of President Kennedy's assassination came over the loud speaker, I was slouching at a Formica table in the junior high school cafeteria in Floral Park Memorial High School, completing my hour of imprisonment in seventh grade study hall. My friend Vincent Alonso sat across from me, and, when we heard the shocking report of the tragic shooting in Dallas, our eyes connected. We both smiled—the kind of sickening, uncomfortable smile that only surfaces when the news is hard and the right response isn't ready on tap—the enigmatic smile. I'll always remember Vinnie for that.

But on a summer day in 1991 when I heard the news of my nephew's accident, there was no enigmatic response. Suddenly I became aware of my body, the need to draw breath through a windpipe that had narrowed, chest walls that didn't want to move, and legs that seemed to buckle under my own weight. This moment became a frozen frame, a mind tattoo that will flash for the rest of my life whenever I peel carrots.

* * * * * * *

It's July, and the high desert air shimmers with heat. I'm standing at the kitchen sink of our shabby rental house in Lakeview preparing vegetables for dinner. The kitchen's cramped and cluttered with dirty dishes and the ephemera of life with children. The countertops are held together with duct tape, and a painted cement floor flakes red chips of latex contributing to the room's oppressive ambiance.

A cloudy kitchen window looks out on an unkempt backyard with giant cottonwoods and overgrown weeds. Our dog, Brock, broods in the shade, chained to one of the massive trees.

"It's time to pick up after the dog and mow," I think as I survey the yard from my post at the sink, but I dismiss the thought. Addressing the mess would be overwhelming in the stifling heat. It will have to wait.

My visiting mother-in-law, Dee, is reading a novel on the couch in the strip of a living room at the front of our small ranch style home. She's been visiting for almost a week, and things have been tense. The old house steams, and we're both wilting. The kids bounce from one activity to the next, and their noisy interruptions crackle our sense of well-being. I've retreated to the kitchen for some space. I don't know how to make Dee's visit more positive.

When the phone rings, I rinse the strips of carrot peel off my hands and turn away from the sink to answer.

My sister-in-law's voice doesn't waiver. Her words tumble from the phone in faint staccato, as if from a far off place: "There's been an accident on Mt. Hood. Johnny fell and hit his head. He's brain dead."

In this instant, time breaks into before and after. Mundane issues that so consumed our thoughts and activities on that sweltering summer afternoon fall like the vegetable peelings in the sink. I run to my mother-in-law to hold her close. No news could ever be this bad. Fourteen-year-old Johnny will never grow up. He will complete his time on this planet as an organ donor.

* * * * * * *

As a nurse I'd taken care of several patients who were donors. They sometimes came to our floor on respirators for palliative care until transplants could be arranged. Once active, full of youth and vigor, they lingered, the tender light of conscious life gone. Irreversible damage to the structures of the brain as evidenced by the cessation of spontaneous breathing and other vital reflexes, lack of response to stimuli, absent muscle activity, and a flat electroencephalogram (EEG) over time—this was the donor's plight.

As I cared for these patients, I thought about their brief lives—their desires, plans, and futures all snuffed out on a quick motorcycle ride to a friend's house or on a car trip to the mall. Most had suffered serious head injuries and their often unblemished bodies, soon to be dissected for organs, looked so normal. I yearned to have it all undone. I sought some sign of consciousness, a glimmer of humanity, a spark of spirit that would prove the brain tests wrong.

I saw so many families of comatose patients do this—grasp at every flicker of an eyelash or reflexive twitch, searching their loved ones' faces with frank longing as they struggled to accept the inevitable. They looked at me with hopeful eyes asking for validation.

"Paul tried to open his eyes today, nurse. Mildred saw it," one father said as his eyes met mine begging for a response.

We both gazed down at his son's pale form in the hospital bed as his respirator pistons pumped. I didn't speak. I didn't have to. Instead I smoothed his son's amber hair and adjusted his patient gown. Pain was etched into the father's face despite his hopeful words. What passed between us was a sort of leaden reality that by-passed the cerebrum and went straight for the gut.

One day on the job, I found myself alone in the room with a dark, extremely handsome donor. He rested on his back, his jet black hair splayed pompadour-like on the pillow which gave him the look of a sleeping Elvis. Still too young to shave, his tawny skin, smooth and beautiful, glowed with youth. An endotracheal tube, taped in his mouth and attached to a machine to make him breathe, was the only indication of his sad situation.

Although at this time I had no children of my own, I thought of his mother. How hard it would be to see a young child in such a state—brain non-functioning, hopes dashed—such an awful loss with no consolation. The boy slept on, unaware and sadly silent, ventilator pumping, waiting to serve and give his final beautiful gift of life to someone in need.

As we rushed to Portland on that fateful day our little family saw the news of Johnny's death glaring through the glass of the newspaper machine outside a coffee shop. It broadcasted information we already knew was coming, but its finality hit hard. Some of us cried openly, others sobbed in private alcoves. Although we reached out to each other, there was a void that nothing could fill. Life had changed. Nothing could make it right.

As I stood by my nephew's casket in the funeral home, I

noticed the dark stitches at the end of the long incision made to harvest his organs peeking out from under the collar of his white shirt. I thought of his sweet persona as a little child in blue velvet shorts and vest at my wedding as he held onto his mother's dress and ran in the grass of my mother-in-law's yard under the gorgeous backdrop of the Rocky Mountains. I thought of the people who might get his liver, his heart, his beautiful eyes with their long lashes. This wasn't what we'd planned.

I remembered Johnny as a young teen, so full of life, energy, and enthusiasm, jumping off the deck onto his backyard trampoline. I pictured the man he might have grown up to become and rued how little effort I'd made to spend time with him. I spoke to his dead form, his empty tent, to express my sorrow and repent of my selfishness. Regret echoing in a tiny chamber at the back of a funeral home. This is one definition of grief.

Weeks later at the wedding of a friend's daughter, Tom and I heard the story of a couple who months earlier found their fourteen-year-old son strangled in a twisted hammock. We spied those parents across the room. No one needed to point them out. My husband and I felt their loss like a mysterious vapor wafting our way. It moved without words and tugged at us to connect. Our grief for our Johnny was still fresh, and we hadn't found even a glimmer of peace. We knew a mere sliver of what those parents were feeling. All the while we wished we didn't.

* * * * * * *

It's late at night, almost two decades since Johnny died, and my husband and I are sitting by the bed of his elderly mother in a cubicle in the intensive care unit of her small town hospital in Steamboat Springs. Blinking monitors cast an eerie glow in the windowless room with a single glass wall looking out on a narrow hall. Dee lies on her back in a standard blue-and-white checked gown tethered to the bed by wires and tubes. In and out of consciousness, she struggles with confusion.

Her mind floats, suspended in a fuzzy reality that defies her to make sense of her surroundings. Scenes from her long life jumble in a whirling collage as she speaks of people and places of the past. She's lost track of what's happened to her and doesn't know where she is. Nothing makes sense. Something's blocking connections she once took for granted, wreaking havoc with her perception.

Dee fingers the tubing coming from the needles in her arm as if adjusting a bracelet. She reaches up with detached interest and rakes my hair to remove invisible treasures. As an avid traveler well into her eighties, her mind alternately resides in places she once visited: Vietnam, Liverpool, and Sri Lanka. The flowers on the wallpaper border across from the bed move like football players on a field. She's lost her bearings, and, although she doesn't know our names, she looks to Tom and me for help.

Tom and I are not typical family visitors. The setting and routines of a hospital are way too familiar—fused into our DNA. We understand medical jargon and know what sedatives to ask for, what tests to refuse, and how to assess the quality of Dee's care. Our vigilance is tiring. We question every decision and never rest. We have too much knowledge. At the same time, we realize that our relationship with Dee might taint our objectivity. It's all very disconcerting.

I gently ease Dee down as she rises up to get out of bed.

"Try to get some rest, Dee. You're in the hospital, and you're very sick."

She stares at me with panic in her eyes.

"I feel like a stranger in a foreign land," she gasps. "I don't know the customs, what's expected."

The truth comes out and I can identify.

"It's a foreign land for both of us," I tell her as I adjust her crumpled pillow and smooth the hair from her eyes. The role of caring for a relative in intensive care is new territory—another side of nursing. I'm learning as I go.

Days after Dee's admission to intensive care, the doctors

drew Tom and me into a room to view his mother's X-rays. The results of numerous scans were clipped end-to-end on a lighted panel that ran the length of one wall. Dee was no stranger to this hospital. Increasing problems with equilibrium and numerous falls, up to this point attributed to old age, had led to several head injuries and broken bones over a period of years. But the X-ray storyboard finally revealed the source of her chronic disequilibrium and current confusion. A hidden tumor was shifting her brain, sabotaging its connections. Whether cancerous or not, it was inoperable.

When we returned to ICU, the sedative the nurse had given Dee was finally kicking in. Our patient slept quietly in perfect repose. Her face, lined with years of living, looked peaceful, even beautiful. I felt the need to study it.

As I sat by her bedside I imagined my mother-in-law as a young woman on the streets of New York with her quick stride and active mind. I remembered our first meeting when she barely glanced my way, pointing to the silverware drawer with a brisk order to set the table. I recalled a moment in 1971 when I stood in her living room and we embraced for the first time, sharing the knowledge of our mutual love for her son. I heard her laugh as my daughter laughs, with a childlike delight in her own insightful humor and saw her standing by the open refrigerator in her kitchen, all business, concocting an awful soup out of Thanksgiving leftovers—dumping lime Jell-O, cranberry sauce, pickles, olives, and shreds of curled turkey skin into a stew pot, adding boiling water, and calling the family to lunch. I thought of her powerful personality housed in a petite body and her sometimes terse way of communicating that often masked a supremely generous spirit.

The suffering of sickness can sometimes snuff out the light of personality, but Dee's spark was spared. The spunk that rolled with the roiling waves of life, that always rose to meet the challenge of whatever the days dealt, rose to the occasion once again. Medication soon cleared some of the fog, and she was partially back. We moved her to a room in the nursing home attached to the hospital, and she settled in.

"Do you ever get thirsty?" Dee asked. My husband looked at me. A glass of water with a straw sat on her bedside table within easy reach. She knew that there was an issue—she was parched—but she couldn't determine what to do about it. Problem solving eluded her. What if she needed the bathroom? She had no use for the call light and was too woozy to get up on her own. Her memory was shot and a quick tutorial had no effect. It was obvious that we couldn't leave her alone.

I saw the fear in Dee's face as I pushed her wheelchair up to the table in the nursing home cafeteria. Her eyes darted as she fumbled with the silverware, trying to remember the routine. Things that used to be done by rote now took concentration. She added salt to her water, stirred her food with a knife, and looked to me for validation as she put her straw in the mashed potatoes and crumbled toast into her coffee. On some level she sensed her errors. She was perpetually unsure.

Dee's appetite was a runaway train as a result of heavy doses of steroids, and she couldn't get enough fuel. I sat close to her in the dining hall, directing the food to her mouth and helping her stay on task. One day the stress of the communal eating area overwhelmed her and she whispered in a barely audible voice, "It's time to eat in my room."

Dee was well-known, and many friends and acquaintances stopped by to say hello. As a respected editor of the small town newspaper for many years, she'd touched the lives of people of all ages and walks of life. She looked like her old self and could still carry on a one-sided conversation. Although every eager face was just another stranger, she didn't let it show.

Unable to organize her thoughts for more than a few sentences, but always gracious, she fell back on her once accomplished interviewing skills and greeted each well-wisher with a cheerful, "So tell me about your plans for your life." This would work for a while—people like to talk about themselves.

But as the conversation lulled, she asked again, and again, and again, until most visitors ran out of coherent things to say and made a beeline for the exit.

In her private alcove at the nursing home, we spent many afternoons singing. She remembered the tunes and the words to "Tennessee Waltz" and "Smoke Gets in Your Eyes," two songs of love lost. She was thirty-five years old, raising five young children when her husband left. It was an acrimonious parting that cut deep, and the rejection and bitter sorrow of that experience darkened her spirit for over half a century, tainting family weddings, graduations, and the like with the ominous specter of an accidental meeting of her ex that would spark acidic wrath. Even in her confusion she continued to convey the pain of her husband's betrayal and the abandonment that scarred her. She mourned, still trying to come to terms with a heavy burden of unresolved grief. I've come to know that this is the work of the very old—the letting go of baggage before the final trip.

And I mourned, too—for Dee's lost dream and the bitter roots and poison anger that replaced it; for my husband and his brothers and sisters who saw their father leave and never felt as sure of love again; and for the bitter fallout of that divorce so long ago that had left it's imprint on my own life. I grieved for the decade of my twenties, lost to waiting, wondering, and wanting—caught in the eddy of an on-again-off-again relationship that seemed determined to sap my emotional strength. Regrets in the back of a room at a nursing home—this is another definition of grief.

Though her spirit remained vibrant, the tumor continued to take Dee's memory. Although we'd known each other for almost forty years, she repeatedly asked my name and marveled at the service I provided. I was the mother of three of her grandchildren and her youngest son's wife, but in her jumbled mind I was a kindly nurse, no more. As we spend the long, drawn-out days together, she looked at me with doleful eyes, speaking often of how grateful she was for my care. I keep these special moments in my heart.

I drew her close, inspired by her acceptance of dependence and overcome with admiration of her spirit. Although always fiercely independent, she freely relinquished her hold on control to willing caregivers. Too weak to lift herself off the toilet, she held her arms out for me to boost her up and into a wheelchair. Lying in a hospital bed, surrounded by friends she didn't recognize, she gracefully accepted a temple and foot massage, the offer of a chocolate bunny, and the precious gifts of lifelong friends pouring out love in the form of food and time. During one massage she casually remarked, "These will go down as my blessing days."

On a warm evening in August, just four months before her collapse, Dee and I were standing together on the grass at the reception for my son's wedding. The evening darkness was just descending. The summer air was sweet smelling and balmy, and lights twinkled around the reception tables amidst a floral landscape of the wedding gardens. It had been a glorious day of ceremony and celebration, but Dee was tired. Her tiny frame leaned against me, the as-yet-undiagnosed brain tumor having its effect on her balance and strength. Despite her weakness, she was still herself.

In the background my husband sang a blessing for the dancing newlyweds. They were radiant, gliding along a dance floor glittering with lights, their happiness flowing with the sway of the music to reach out and touch everyone gathered to listen and drink in the beautiful scene. Dee's body listed towards me, and I held her close. She spoke about death; she told me that hers was coming. My heart sank. Somehow I knew this was true.

"Your love has meant so much to us," I said "It's passed through Tom and me on to our family and into the next generation, and we are so grateful. It will never end." Dee glowed with my words, and we hugged with a familiar closeness, as tender as the moment decades ago when our relationship first began in earnest, on the day we recognized that we both loved her son.

Much to my shame and eternal regret I was not there for my parents at the end of their lives. Young and fearful, I couldn't face their pain and dependency and was more into myself. Although I'd been a nurse for many years when they died, I had no spiritual moorings and had become adept at avoiding feelings as a way to cope. The sting of death was something I didn't want to face. But remarkably, through the courageous last days of my frail mother-in-law's life, I was finally able to face death head-on.

When Dee passed on in my fifty-sixth year, the fear was gone. I felt at peace. I'd come to believe that this life is not all there is. Death has lost its sting. The Bible tells me so.

Chapter 25

Power

"All things flow, nothing abides."

Heraclitus

Riding home in the car after a weekend retreat with friends, no one's talking. Laptop keys click, fingers caress handheld screens, camera cards unload, and every person, except the driver, is engrossed in his or her own little world. Occasionally tender souls will glance up from their glowing screens to acknowledge something that's been said, but, after a brief nod, their bobbing heads snap back as if attached to the computer by short elastic cords to return their attention to tasks that seem much more important. Rarely do eyes meet. Gone are the lively conversations and serendipitous connections of road trips of the past. I feel alone.

It's no secret that American culture lauds rugged individualism at the expense of community. The internet, and its constant intrusion into the sacred spaces of connection, tacitly assures that all our interactions with others will be on our own terms. Computers consume more and more of our brief vaporous time on this earth, taunting us into scandal and devouring hours in the pursuit of information that can be just so much chasing after the wind. I sense the curmudgeonly tendencies that cause me to wax poetic about the old days and this is my conundrum. I know there's no going back.

* * * * * * *

On an ordinary day in 2006 working as an RN in an assisted living facility, I finally made the decision to stop working as a nurse. At the not so tender age of fifty-seven, I joined the ranks of millions of retired nurses and left the profession.

I slipped out of nursing in much the same way I chose it—in an instant and without much forethought. It happened on a regular day as I went about business as usual. I entered the room of a one-hundred-year-old man preparing to give him a dose of vitamin B-12, unaware of the momentous decision that lay ahead.

My patient sat in a wheelchair gazing out the window of his small apartment onto a parking lot below. He was a tall, once handsome man with a gentle personality. Like so many of his peers, his days had been reduced to waiting for meals, meds, and brief visits from family and staff. His health was waning and his energy with it. Time weighed heavy. He rarely left his room because he was embarrassed about his appearance.

On the day in question, he was in the mood to talk. He recounted the story of his long and rich life, beginning with a teenage decision to take a position as a clerk in a small town shoe store, later becoming its owner. He married, had five children, and spent his days helping the town's people find shoes for the work, the weddings, and the wakes of their lives. The store closed in 1975, a victim of globalization and the self-serve shoe-bins at big-box retail outlets, but his shoe store stories remained for sharing, and his cloudy eyes seemed less so as he told them.

When it came time to administer the injection, I did what I had done literally thousands of times before. Because the patient had very little fat or muscle tissue, the needle went in hard, and I had to push more than usual to get the medication to leave the syringe. I could see the pain in my elderly patient's eyes. I felt the shot hurting more than it would ever help, and my lack of faith in what I was doing turned my stomach.

Suddenly I was *sick* of invasive procedures, the tubes, the tests, the tedious protocols, paperwork, and pill pushing. An irresistible urge hit like a bolt of lightning. Some of my patients weren't much older than me, and micromanaging their care was my job. This wasn't how I wanted to spend the years I had left. Leaving nursing behind promised a freedom that seemed as real as claiming a new life. Why hadn't I moved on years ago? Why hadn't I done it when I first felt the pinch of a profession that never felt quite comfortable? The fact that I would hang up my non-existent nursing cap in a place that most people consider the end of the line seemed so fitting.

Despite the finality of my decision on that day, I knew that I would always be a nurse. The boundaries between me and hurting people, often filmy and easily breeched, had undergone a momentous shift. Unafraid to touch or to be touched, I often sense sorrow blipping between me and others on an invisible radar screen that had been fine-tuned over the years. Legions need a healing word of connection and recognition of their suffering. So many people are lonely and want someone to listen. Very often I feel lonely, too.

Even though I'm no longer employed as a nurse at the nursing home, I find myself drawn back there. There I don't feel so alone. It seems an odd place to find solace—the privation there so stark and unmistakable. Elderly residents—most who have ceded their homes, health, and autonomy—rest in chairs around the periphery of big rooms, staring vacantly, often dozing with only time to spend. Their awards and ribbons are nowhere to be seen and titles are rarely acknowledged. Most of the accoutrements of their worldly lives have been offered up and forgotten. Those that remain have lost their importance.

A university professor, masterful leader of thousands of musical concerts over decades, sits quietly now, slumped in his wheelchair listening with his clouded mind to an elevator music sound track that plays without mercy. Star athletes with withered faces lounge in recumbent wheelchairs, no longer moving. Lauded community servants and leaders recline idly and wait to be served. Committee chairmen of yesteryear voice no opinions and make no decisions. Aged mothers hug dolls.

The outside world spins without these people. The places where they labored for decades—the offices, schools, hospitals, and factories—went on to hire others, who now claim innovations as their own, largely without looking back to the achievements or struggles of the past. Stacks of once carefully-considered policy manuals, housed in plastic three-ring binders representing years of work, deteriorate in dingy basement archives. Many friends have gone on to other places. They've died or moved out-of-state. Important meetings have been reduced to decisions about medical care. Children long ago set sail on their own adventures. Even the treasured possessions of youth have been discarded: the gilded serving bowls, cut crystal vases, and silver-plated trays—wedding gifts from cherished loved ones in the 1940's and 50's—now languish at church rummage sales. They're out of style.

It may be hard to understand what I see in this shabby enclave at the end of the hall with its dull floors, putrid smells, and out-of-tune piano. Elderly patients with filmy eyes seem to see realities that healthy minds can't visualize. Alarms blare and grate as residents, tethered for safety, attempt to rise from confinement. Moans escape and helplessness cries out, unhidden. The losses are in your face.

But pity has no place here. Pity flows in one direction to separate the visitor from the visited, and no matter what our age or condition, connection is what we need, and mercy is a two-way street. Of course, some encounters are staged, full of chit-chat about the weather, mindless clichés, and forced cheerfulness, but a few visits bloom with sincerity and spirits touch. I can't shake the awareness that my friend's fate may one day be my own. Even in the wrenching silence of Alzheimer's, this awareness is a gift.

An elderly resident approaches. She speaks with frank sincerity. "What kind of hotel is this with all these ponies? Why have we come to this circus?" Her eyes search mine.

I give her the only answer that seems right. "I don't know, Evelyn, we're just here for a short time."

Suddenly I'm acutely aware that all we have is this moment, this seemingly meaningless interaction between two human souls, so mundane, yet so pregnant with sisterhood. Despite the nursing facility's less-than-ideal ambiance, people are approachable there. The communication is frank, frequently non-verbal, and without hidden agendas. No one's wielding power or jockeying for position. The desires of many of the aged are muted if not gone. Trophies have no meaning.

"Will you wear a bikini the next time you come?" Lois asks, her marbled eyes looking in my direction.

The image this comment evokes appalls me, and I laugh. Lois's eyes brighten, and there's a clear connection between us.

"No, it's against the law," I say, embarrassed to even think of what that would look like. Vanity keeps me from a type of freedom Lois knows.

The vulnerability of loss brings this bounty. It hones life down to its essential parts, uncovering the all-pervasive illusion of our immortality. It lays bare our "not knowing" in a world that tells us that knowledge is power and that we are in control. It helps us to see what is so often hidden to the world of the well—that our independence is an illusion. The only things that are of lasting importance are the things Jesus calls the "blessings of the poor in spirit," the unseen things. The residents' weaknesses allow me to see this truth.

Fifty-three year-old Sally's dying. She's suffering on the morning I came to the nursing care center, plagued with a serious headache. Like my mother-in-law, her brain's muddled by an encroaching tumor that can't be excised, garbling the thoughts she expresses and limiting her understanding. As tears formed in the corners of Sally's eyes, hovered, and slowly rolled down her cheeks, the staff reassured her that help was near, as close as the strong narcotic she'd just swallowed and in the love of all those who have gathered around to hold her hand and wipe the teardrops before they fell. God is love, and, as we ministered to her weakness, I felt His presence.

This concept remains a hard sell for the world at large. The three "Es" of education, employment, and estate consume and define our lives. They eat our time and tell us who we are but rarely address the question of meaning at all.

A friend's experiences mirror these sentiments. Her daughter was recovering from injuries in an auto accident. Alone with her grief and weary from the emotional demands of her daughter's care, my friend found solace among the alcoholics and junkies on break from a rehab class, catching smokes in front of the hospital. Pride stood humbled there, and, in its stead, came a meekness born from the bitter bite of experience—the knowledge of one's powerlessness. There my friend felt free to cry, talk, smoke, and pace with others who also felt weak, alone, and lost. In this place she found a kind of peace. There she found her religion.

As I did in my early years, many seekers choose to fashion their own faith. They're suspicious of traditional church dogma and confident they'll find their own way. A politically-tainted version of Christianity, mocked by the media, turns many people off. Looking for something new, they glom onto New Age ideas that are hot for a time and then gone. The watered down, ever-changing, individualized religions that result from dabbling at the spiritual buffet frequently seem more like fashionable fads than spiritual truth, and the deep significance of the sacred teachings and traditions is thus lost. Like I did during my twenties and early thirties, many people dismiss the Bible as outdated without acknowledging the centuries of diligent work done by seekers and saints of the past. Accepting the Bible's message seems like giving up too much. Precious independence and choice have become new gods.

Giant retail franchises sell secularized Bible verses on wooden plaques. "What a nice saying," the clerk at the checkout says, unaware of its biblical origins. Massive crucifixes, long a fashion statement, seem to be everywhere. The woman at the jewelry counter of a large department store asks, "Do you want a plain one, or one with a little man on it?"

In her memoir, *Growing in Circles*, Bonnie L. Casey writes of struggling to make peace with God. Raised in the Adventist Church, she remembers being urged to spend "a thoughtful hour each day contemplating the sacrifice of Christ." Bonnie writes: "I was fairly certain that holding a mental image of a particularly barbaric form of torture would not bring me the kind of peace I sought."

By her own admission, Bonnie doesn't see as I see. The absurd paradoxes—the weak as strong, the foolish as wise, the despised as blessed, and the last becoming first, (the Sermon on the Mount in summary)—are all demonstrated by Jesus on the cross.

Eugene Kennedy writes in his book *Cardinal Bernardin's Stations of the Cross*:

> "...all the sorrows of time, all the bloodied hands dripping iron bars, all the arms bearing wasted and dying children, all the backs bent and scarred by unjust punishments, all the terrified eyes glimpsed as boxcar doors slide shut, all the sweet-faced youth stunned into blank staring death on muddy fields, all those taken down by heartbreak, all those crying against the sky for losses too great to bear or too small to name, all those whose gifts are never even opened, and

> all those denied even a taste of the battered,
> bittersweet glory of being human–for all these
> Jesus intones his lament in a desperate call from
> the cross that finishes His Father's work by
> braiding our sorrows into His own."

The cross reveals the abject nature of our metaphysical desires for power, money, and prestige—things that will not last. It tells us that the victim is the Lord and shows us love without conditions. The cross tears our world apart.

It has torn mine.

Chapter 26

❧

Coincidential Oppositorum

"I speak of unremarkable forces that split the heart and make the pavement toss—forces concealed in quiet people and plants. If we are conditioned to respond to noise and size—we will miss God."

George Meredith

Cows graze behind the supermarket and wheat fields roll for miles on one side of the alley behind the shopping center in the town where I live. It's a lonely strip of road—a soothing respite from the traffic and frenetic activity of the parking lot in front of the stores. Drivers are discouraged from taking this route by a series of lofty speed bumps installed to assure that cars won't clog the delivery lane. This uneven pavement forces a slower pace and provides a kind of rhythm to the journey. As I drive down this alley, I slow down to ease the car over each asphalt hump, anticipating the jolt to come. It's relaxing. I like knowing what to expect.

The conspicuous evidence of consumption litters this corridor. Stacks of wooden pallets, torn shrink wrap, and plastic strapping bands lay discarded—the common refuse of retail operations. Battered dumpsters with Smurf-colored paint, bulging with cardboard and packing peanuts, rest against the drab cinderblock walls that form the backside of the marketplace we call the mall. Big Box bandits, spewing cardboard and clamshell plastic, operate out of step with the rhythms of the natural world.

The peaceful pasture that lies on the other side of this alley seems out of place. This bucolic scene soothes, a stark contrast to the commercial setting that is its backdrop. Threatened by the encroaching ooze of molten asphalt that will permanently harden it into a tarry tomb, the meadow currently teems with life. These parallel scenes clash.

As I begin the slow traverse of this undulating path, I'm lost in thought. The alley is quiet—no traffic today. I turn the radio to classical music. The piece is lilting and lovely.

Without warning, hundreds of small black birds descend on my car. Swirling, whipping, and whirling, they snake towards me and then away in long symmetrical streams, forming layers of concentric black rings. As if hearing the music, they twirl and sweep like ribbons in the wind, circling the car in syncopated rhythm. They move with my automobile as I continue down the alley, and, as quickly as they came, they vanish as if sucked by a celestial vacuum that also sucks my breath away.

I negotiate the last speed bump, still thinking about what just happened, and turn onto the street to head for home. As the car tires hit the pavement, a radio announcer speaks clearly: "You have been listening to a composition by the French composer Ravel written in 1904, entitled *Oiseaux Tristes* (The Unhappy Birds).

This is a sublime moment of *coincidential oppositorum*: things that seem separate, coinciding to reveal an unexpected unity that transforms an ordinary drive down a littered alley into something out of this world—the intersection of the yin and the yang, the good and the bad, the complimentary colors that sing, the contrast that makes art pop. The spiritual world comes down to intersect our worldly plane. Philosophers call it synchronism, dreamers claim coincidence, and mystics see God's intervention. Whatever the description, the massive tapestry that is life seldom reveals its golden pattern except in rare glimpses of something spiritual—the holy.

The world says seeing is believing, but the Bible tells us believing is seeing. We know the birds, the wheat fields, and junky strip behind the mall because we see them with our eyes. All of these may be here today but could be gone tomorrow. Yet just as real are the unseen things—the invisible things that the Bible tells us are eternal. And this unseen world often breaks through when we least expect it, in the places we can't fix or understand—when we're not in control—when we don't know it all.

* * * * * * *

On a quiet afternoon in July at a Joni and Friends retreat for families affected by disability, I pushed an eight-year-old girl in a wheelchair on a paved walkway through the redwoods of the camp grounds. It was the end of my very first session at the camp and a certain weariness was affecting my spirit. My camper had a serious disability, and the week caring for her, which allowed her parents and sister to have time to enjoy camp, had proved taxing. I'd been running non-stop all week barely taking the time to wolf down my food. My feet were hurting. I'd lost a few pounds.

My charge for the week was a sweet round-faced girl named Sarah, who was severely affected by a genetic condition called Angelman's Syndrome resulting from a problem on her 15th chromosome. (The mutation is on the same chromosome that caused Natalie's condition, but in a different place.) Sarah's expressive and interpretive language were both gravely impaired and communication proved difficult. Even nonverbal cues and sign language seemed to have little or no meaning for her.

Although her vision was clouded by cataracts, Sarah could run, and she scurried around the camp holding her bent arms over her head, hands flapping like a "happy puppet," which happens to be another name to describe the incurable condition she'd had since birth. Keeping her safe required constant vigilance. The activities of the children's program, which included coloring, arts and crafts, and games, were beyond her ability as she seemed unaware of her own acts of intention. The wheelchair ride through the redwoods was as much a break for me for me as it was fun for her—a moment of respite where she was contained and entertained. I desperately needed a rest. I felt in awe of the commitment her parents made to care for her at home. After five days, I was spent.

As we walked through the trees, Sarah's mother turned toward me.

"I don't believe all the Christian rhetoric I'm hearing at this camp." she said, her face scrunched, voice tinged with anger. "We've been here for almost a week, and some of these professed Christians don't treat my daughter with anything that looks like love."

I paused, not exactly sure how to respond because I knew her words *might* be true. Christian hypocrisy is one thing atheists and agnostics are right about. The world tugs at us all. It's hard for everyone, Christian or not, to see past the values that rule the day telling everyone that the worth of a person is determined by what they do. Sarah's disability will preclude her from almost every parameter society uses to measure success and value. She will never hold a job, earn a college degree, or live on her own. As I turned to face her hurting mother, I was overcome with compassion.

"People will always fail you, Joan." I said with affection. "So many people look at Christians and fail to see Jesus. We're all so flawed. Only God is perfect."

Although definitely not a singer, I succumbed to the urge to belt out a tune. I began to sing the words of an old hymn:

Turn your eyes upon Jesus
Look full in His wonderful face.
And the things of this world will grow strangely dim
In the light of His glory and grace.

As I sang this old hymn, little Sarah, her handicapping condition so severe as to prevent communication and understanding, spread her arms wide overhead, tilted her head back, and looked up.

For most of my life, these kinds of holy moments went unnoticed and were beyond my ability to perceive or name what was happening. I had no eyes to see. My journey toward sight began as a plebe in nursing school standing by the Stryker frame of a paralyzed girl, when I felt some of her pain. An unseen force hit the day I hugged a grieving woman by the dairy case in Safeway, and I saw myself in her brokenness. It broke through when I felt Cindy's anger and her powerlessness as she lay trapped in her massive, obese body and knew that I felt trapped too. It took me by surprise as I sat on the roof of a house in north Idaho rocking my little son, overcome with wonder and relief; and when I met my daughter Natalie's eyes as she lay on a hospital gurney awaiting surgery, my tears mingling with hers as we suffered together. All of this and so much more was a gift.

I now know that a nurse's story is chiefly one of gift. A chance to stand with the sick in their sadness and to share the vulnerability of their pain, and thus to have a glimpse of something beyond—a shimmering flicker of the mystery that's so often missed in the busy commerce of worldly life. The holy.

These instances of insight bring to mind one other holy moment. On the cross, where Jesus cried out, "My God, my God, why have you forsaken me?"

At that point of *coincidential oppositorium*, total abandonment and total brokenness touched total acceptance and love. In that instant, a gift to the world was given, and in powerlessness it was received.

When life is impacted by illness and suffering, we frequently have no other choice but to let go. That's when we have the opportunity to choose the faith demonstrated by Jesus—the faith that the Bible describes—a faith that brings the promise that pain will have meaning, that love and faithfulness will come together, and that as the bible says, "righteousness and peace will kiss." And we have the promise of a life that will last beyond this world. Though we see only through a glass darkly now, someday we will understand.

Chapter 27

❧

Going Back

For us who nurse, our nursing is a thing which, unless we are making progress every year, every month, every week, take my word for it, we are going back. "

Florence Nightingale

It's the summer of 2012, and I've popped into a hospital to visit my friend. Tanya's resting comfortably in a private room recovering from surgery for colon cancer. Machines surround her bed recording her heart rate, blood pressure, and oxygen levels. She administers her own pain medication with a pump attached to her IV, which is monitored by a machine around the clock. Her sister has been spending the night in a recliner at the bedside to tend to Tanya's comfort and to help her get to the bathroom.

A nurse with a badge bops into the room to administer antibiotics from a pre-filled syringe that has been prepared and labeled by a hospital pharmacist, and she uses an electronic device to scan the barcode on Tanya's wristband as well as the one on the syringe before she administers the dose. A large computer is mounted on the wall by the head of the bed, and its screen holds the nurse's attention for the better part of half an hour as she documents her patient's condition and care. Tanya is on the receiving end of state-of-the art medical technology in a modern private hospital in the United States of America. Her nurse is caring for two post-op patients on her shift and seems unharried. Before leaving the room, she advises her patient to use the bedside spirometer to expand her lungs. It's only been two days since surgery, but, because Tanya's operation was done through a small incision in her bellybutton, she is expected to go home tomorrow.

The hallway outside the patient's room is quiet. No doctors hectoring. No frantic nurses with worried looks bolting past with bulky carts full of syringes and solutions to mix. No blood draws and IV starts by staff nurses on the fly, or RNs flailing down the hall wielding respiratory therapy equipment and suction machines. No one's timing intravenous fluids with a wristwatch, let alone administering thirty or more bottles of IV fluid every shift as we did at County General so many years ago. A lot of patient care has been outsourced to family, modern machinery, and a plethora of medical specialists.

Gone are the days of routine six-inch abdominal incisions, six-bed wards, and sixty medications to mix from powder. Gone are the clipboards of patient data at the foot of each bed, hit-or-miss charting, china markers to label syringes, and the giant roster of hourly care tacked to a wall in the hallway with a checklist for each patient's bed-bath, oral care, and backrub, even if there doesn't seem to be time. Gone is the era of the do-it-all-and-then-some nurse with twenty-seven patients under her care. These have all gone the way of the typewriter.

But some things haven't changed. Cancer still kills. Weeks after my visit, Tanya's doctors tell her that her cancer has metastasized beyond the point of effective treatment.

A nurse holds Tanya's hand as she receives this grim news. A nurse is there to listen and help on the day Tanya enters into hospice care. A nurse stands by her side as she takes her last breath.

* * * * * * *

Over forty years have passed since my husband and I first set foot in County General Hospital. On a whim, we've decided to return. The sun blazes as we pull up to a row of duplexes on a narrow side street across from what is now a sprawling urban medical center. Identical tarpaper shanties line one side of this street and they comfort us. Although now dwarfed by snarls of overgrown weeds, they look much as they did in the 1970s when we parked our Volkswagens in front of them before heading to work. Decades later their crumbling facades are a welcome sight because, like old friends, they remind us that we're back. It isn't just a dream.

But nothing else looks familiar. Construction cranes beep to warn those in their path as they plunge ahead in the lots across from those old homes splaying a film of dust into dry air. Workers call out to each other in Spanish. The atmosphere is choked with car exhaust and summer heat. The loud drone of traffic and heavy machinery heightens our feeling of being on edge.

As Tom and I maneuver ourselves around the plywood barriers that surround the construction site, we realize that we're not sure where to go. Brick buildings tower and we squint into the bright sky straining to make out the shell of the old hospital—a place we once knew so well. Swarms of people hurry in and out of various doors, and eventually we opt for one that seems right.

Outpatients wait in wheelchairs, and their families mill around a central area decorated in terrcotta tile. We recognize this space. It's the old County emergency room. It seems strange to see the transformation—uncomfortable. I feel like a voyeur checking out an old boyfriend on the sly. I identify with the people waiting. I, too, am now often a patient on the receiving end of care.

My heart thumps as we take a familiar elevator to the seventh floor. I sense it beating in my throat but feel strangely detached. This is an Alfred Hitchcock moment—a still-life frame caught between curiosity and dread, the world of the present and the past, a chance to enter a time machine. The elevator's smaller and tighter than I remember and seems to move with surreal speed. All that's missing is some eerie music.

When the doors open, we step out shoulder-to-shoulder onto a carpeted surface and look around. The décor's been updated, but it's unmistakably the right place. I feel my husband tense. This was the training camp of our youth. He has history here, too.

Suddenly I realize I am an older woman standing where I once stood on a linoleum floor in my twenties leaning on a rolling medicine cart as I was dressed down by a raging resident. The days at County General pass before my eyes like a rapid-fire slide show. My mind strips away the cosmetic changes to the facility, hurling me back to the time when I flew down these same halls with the heavy weight of too much responsibility on my shoulders. My knees buckle, and I lean into my husband and bury my face in his chest. Once again I'm crying.

But it's not a good cry. Not a catharsis. The past is immutable. At times I still feel that awful weight of grief bearing down. Nothing can change what happened here.

A doctor wearing scrubs joins us in the elevator on our way down. He stares intently at a clipboard, tapping his pencil on the metal clip and becomes part of my story. He looks to be twenty-something, sporting a ruddy complexion and wire-rimmed glasses just like Tom's. I tell him that we were once in his shoes: that Tom was a medical student and I was a registered nurse on the surgical floor more than forty years ago. I tell him how nurses took care of twenty-seven patients without much help. I tell him that it was hard.

The kid looks up only briefly and nods, as if politely acknowledging my comments on the weather. He exits on the first floor without a word, never glancing back.

I'm by no means a hero. I'm an ordinary woman. No personal holocaust lurks in my past, no serious family dysfunction aching for redemption. No fame or tragic ill-fortune to add pizzazz and pique the Schadenfreude of the curious. I've never been to war. But this visit to the past has awakened something new. In some small way I feel like a veteran returning from battle with invisible scars of war to face the careless crowd. The struggles I've witnessed and shared during my life as a nurse are a history story that few will ever read, yet they seem important. Finally giving voice to them seems right.

As I pass through the crowded lobby on the way to what's left of the rest of my life, a certain peace descends. My tears are spent. A lot of what happened at County and during my years in the profession has made me who I am today.

I have the impulse to offer it all up.

I will always be a nurse. Stepping through the door out into the bright sunshine, I look up and thank my God.

Chapter 28

❦

The Pearl of Great Price

He has sent Me ...
To comfort all who mourn,
To console those who mourn in Zion
To give them beauty for ashes
The oil of joy for mourning
The garment of praise for the spirit of heaviness.

Isaiah 61:1-3 NIV

A bell jingles in the distance, and my five-year-old mind jumps to attention. I run inside to find my mother who's working in the kitchen of our three-room garden apartment in Flushing. It's the Good Humor ice cream truck offering its frosty treats on the corner, right on schedule. I've been waiting.

My mother hands me a few coins, and I run down the cement steps with a horde of other children streaming from identical pods of brick flats, all headed for the same destination. A very tall man in a white suit and paper hat stands outside a small truck with a familiar logo—a chocolate-covered ice cream bar on a stick. The kids crowd around as he hands out frozen treats in paper cones and puts the money in a coin holder around his waist.

The ice cream's coated with chocolate and tastes of banana, but its sweetness is overshadowed by a precious treasure that's all my own—a Good Humor charm which comes with every purchase. For months I've been collecting these miniature toys in a cylindrical wicker basket. I cherish them.

I hold my latest acquisition in a tight fist. It's a bird peeking out from a broken shell. The chick's faintly-painted eyes peer over the top of the egg's ragged edge, and, holding it, I feel reborn. It joins the others in my stash: a tiny working whistle, a seal balancing on a striped ball, a cowboy on horseback, and a stockpile of zoo animals rendered in pastel plastic. Once home I peruse the assortment with all the passion of an avid collector, sorting and fondling each one. The wicker basket with clasping lid holds all my worldly treasures.

One day I am sitting on the stairs in front of our walk-up. The basket lies open, and I scoop its contents out on warm cement. My tiny toys gleam in the sunlight. I love to handle them.

Suddenly I am aware that someone's watching. A nameless, faceless boy from the neighborhood is standing over me, casting his shadow on my collection. He offers me one of his charms: a pink, plastic clam holding a pearl.

"It's a real pearl," he tells me, "a one-of-a-kind."

He hands me the trinket and I turn it over in my five-year-old hands, feeling its weight and fingering the gem. To make it mine I'll have to relinquish my entire cache. The pearl glistens in its bubble gum colored shell. It's as appealing and delightful as any charm could be.

The decision comes in a flash. With a young child's aplomb, I turn my treasures over to the boy in exchange for the single bauble. He scoops them up and disappears with haste. Then I'm on the run, heading to the house to show my parents, chest thumping as I take the stairs by twos, the plastic shell rattling in my empty basket. I can hear its beauty.

But my mother and father don't share my happiness. They

tell me I've been taken. I've given up too much. Disappointment washes over me. The pearl still glimmers, but it's only a reminder of the loss.

* * * * * * *

Loss is inevitable. It's woven into the fabric of life. Every beginning is an ending; every moment we call the present soon will be the past. Minutes and hours tick away unnoticed. Age creeps up. Things change. A cavalcade of options not chosen slip silently into the slush pile of oblivion—the proverbial "What if?" file that's only examined in the throes of regret. We can't do and have everything.

"I've spent a long time—many hours and nights—trying to figure out the ultimate thing for me, and it's been completely pointless," says Chris, a young soldier, in a PBS film about returning from war. Combat took Chris's innocence and it's left him floundering. "What I need to do," he concludes, "is find something *so* good that all the moments that sucked are worth it."

"Oh Chris," I think, as his deep sadness comes through on the television screen. I haven't seen combat, but I've seen loss. I've felt that all-consuming ache—the longing for something good and beautiful amidst the pain—and I, too, stumbled in the dark, questions unanswered, not knowing where to turn. I've spent a lifetime looking for peace.

Chris may not know it, but there is a blessing buried in his suffering. In his book *Living Prayer,* Robert Benson writes, "Jesus of Nazareth—the most chosen and most blessed and most shared one of us all—was the most broken of us all." We too must be taken: blessed, broken, and shared. Brokenness and loss, in stark contrast to the whole, holds a wonderful truth. Jesus shows us that in giving up, loss becomes gain, weakness becomes strength. Letting go ends in the reception of a glorious hope if we're willing to give our all. It's the only way.

The story of my childhood bargain is a bit of serendipity that shows this truth. It's a modern parable paralleling the Bible's description of the kingdom of God. It's the story of a merchant, who, seeking good pearls, found one beautiful pearl of great price and sold all that he had to buy it. It's a story of faith—giving one's all for the ultimate good. Like the childish trust that led me to want something special, so much so that I was willing to give everything for that treasure, I have embraced the sacred truth of the Bible and devoted my life to Christ.

Perhaps some might think I've been taken, given up too much—forfeited choice, suspended reason, or caved to convention—to find my comfort. But my patients and all my friends at JAF have shown me otherwise. They've shown me the all-encompassing power of God that is perfected in their weakness and vulnerability. They have taught me what it means to love.

I spent years thinking instead of knowing. And to know I had to take the plunge. I had to suffer for and with others. Jesus is alive and present in our world and He asks me to be present too—to experience, share, love, serve and grow.

Not everyone who swims the River Sorrow will see all the good that the Bible promises God will work out of their suffering. Not everyone will feel the joy, or see the glorious redemption of pain that Joni Eareckson Tada has seen during her time on earth. But my faith in Jesus Christ assures me that all is well, that ultimately all loss will be shown for good. Sorrow will be redeemed. We will receive beauty for ashes.

And, after all these years, crossing the River Sorrow, this is what I have come to believe.

Works Cited

Benson, Robert. *Living Prayer*. New York: Jeremy P. Tarcher/ Putnam, 1998. Print.

Buechner, Frederick. *Beyond Words: Daily Readings in the ABC's of Faith*. New York: Harper SanFrancisco, 2004. Print.

Casey, Bonnie L. *Growing in Circles My Struggle to Make Peace With God, Myself, and Just About Everything*. Two Harbors Press, 2009. Print.

Church, Forrest. *Life Lines: Holding on (and Letting Go)*. Boston: Beacon, 1996. 51. Print.

Coyle, Steve. "Our Bodies Like Tents." *Joni and Friends*. Joni Eareckson Tada, n.d. Web. 09 Nov. 012. <http://www.joniandfriends.org/radio/2011/7/6/our-bodies-tents/>.

Eliot, T. S. 122. The Waste Land." *Eliot, T. S. 1922*.

Kennedy, Eugene. *Cardinal Bernardin's Stations of the Cross Transforming Our Grief and Loss into New Life*. New York: St. Martin's, 2003. 130-31. Print.

Lamott, Anne. *Bird by Bird: Some Instructions on Writing and Life.* New York: Anchor, 1995. Print.

Lewis, C. S. *The Problem of Pain.* New York, NY: Harper One, 2001. Print.

Lewis, C. S. The Weight of Glory

Prather, Hugh. *Spiritual Notes to Myself: Essential Wisdom for the 21st Century.* Berkeley, CA: Conari, 1998. Print.

Rilke, Ranier M. "Famous Quotes, Inspirational Quotes, Love Quotes, Funny Quotes, Quotes." *Famous Quotes, Inspirational Quotes, Love Quotes, Funny Quotes, Quotes.* N.p., n.d. Web. 09 Nov. 2012. <http://www.quotationcafe.com/index.jhtml>.

Rowling, J. K., *Harry Potter and the Deathly Hallows.* New York, NY: Arthur A. Levine, 2007.

Spires, Elizabeth. "Matter | Pattern.": *Half a Dozen More, Beginning with "Easter Sunday, 1955" by Elizabeth Spires.* N.p., n.d. Web. 09 Nov. 2012..

BT 732.7 .R538 2013
Richards, Janet, 1950–
Crossing the River Sorrow

3324822R00131

Made in the USA
San Bernardino, CA
24 July 2013